Emotional Literacy

Also available in the Ideas in Action series

Behaviour Management – Tony Swainston

Encouraging Reading – Susan Elkin

Creative Assemblies – Brian Radcliffe

Creating an Inclusive School – Mal Leicester

Effective Learning – Gavin Reid and Shannon Green

Teaching NLP in the Classroom – Kate Spohrer

Implementing Personalised Learning – Reggie Byram

Putting Assessment for Learning into Practice – David Spendlove

Tackling Bullying in Schools – Daniel Guiney

Also available from Continuum

Developing Children's Emotional Intelligence – Shahnaz Bahman and Helen Maffini

Available from Network Continuum

7 Successful Strategies to Promote Emotional Intelligence in the Classroom – Marziyah Panju

Becoming Emotionally Intelligent (2nd edition) – Catherine Corrie

Emotional Intelligence and Enterprise Handbook – Cheryl Buggy

Emotional Literacy

David Spendlove

Ideas in Action

continuum

Continuum International Publishing Group

The Tower Building
11 York Road
London
SE1 7NX

80 Maiden Lane, Suite 704
New York, NY 10038

www.continuumbooks.com

British Library Cataloguing-in-Publication Data
A catalogue record for this book is available from the British Library.

ISBN: 1847064116 (paperback)

Library of Congress Cataloging-in-Publication Data
Spendlove, David.
  Emotional literacy / David Spendlove.
      p. cm. — (Ideas in action)
  ISBN 978-1-84706-411-0 (pbk.)
  1. Affective education. 2. Emotions in children. 3. Emotional intelligence. I. Title.
  LB1073.S64 2009
  370.15'34--dc22

2008034671

Illustrations by Martin Aston
Typeset by Ben Cracknell Studios | www.benstudios.co.uk
Printed and bound in Great Britain by MPG Books, Ltd, Cornwall

Contents

Acknowledgements

To Mum and Dad for naturing me and
Rachel, William, family and friends for nurturing me . . .

Introduction

'The difficult child is the child who is unhappy. He is at war with himself; and in consequence, he is at war with the world.'

A.S. Neill, *Summerhill*

Who is this book for?

By picking up this book you were subconsciously driven by your emotions to do so. The extent to which you continue to read it will also depend upon the extent to which you are emotionally engaged and motivated by the content, and the degree to which you want to understand your own emotions and those of the learners you engage with.

Unfortunately 'emotion' as a topic has suffered something of a bad press in modern society, as we tend to associate it with extremes, cultural difference and a lack of control. However, our emotions are much more subtle and complex than this as they are central to our well-being, everyday thinking and essential to our survival as they guide us by directing and prioritizing our attention.

Ultimately, we are all pilots of our own emotional lives but some people are able to plot better routes than others. Therefore, this book is not just about raising Key Stage or GCSE average scores, although it may well do so. Instead it is about something much more fundamental than this, which is the sustaining, in our pupils, of a lifelong interest in learning while promoting their emotional well-being. It is often quoted that the United Nations Children's Fund placed UK children as the unhappiest in Europe. This book is therefore designed to give all teachers advice, together with practical information for putting into action ideas about developing emotional literacy within their learning environment, as well as opportunities to consider our own emotions as teachers and how these influences change our actions. In doing so the book adopts a generic approach, making it appropriate for all teachers, including school managers, who may wish to coordinate the delivery of emotional literacy strategies across the school. Such strategies, when coordinated, are best delivered in a contextualized way through different subjects, rather than through a discrete activity as part of personal and social development or citizenship. However, at times, some teachers of some subjects may feel uncomfortable in delivering some of the activities, hence the need for a coordinated and mapped approach in each school.

As well as providing activities for students to use in class, the book also provides reflective opportunities for teachers to consider how their own emotions influence their thinking and actions in everyday school situations. In doing so the book draws extensively upon research from a variety of areas including emotion, evolutionary psychology, philosophy, cognitive neuroscience and pedagogy, as well as scholarly work and best practice: presenting the material in a style that is easily digested. As such, the book serves as a good introduction to the topic of emotional literacy and all readers are encouraged to follow up the further reading suggestions at the back of the book.

Emotion in education

If you are of a certain age you probably won't recall emotion, as a topic, playing a formal part in your school life or even being mentioned as part of your teacher training course. Today, however, children's lives are very different and as a result the past decade has seen increasing discussion relating to the place of emotion within education policy and practice. Many schools now place the concepts of emotional literacy, emotional intelligence and emotional well-being at the centre of a child's development. Part of this upsurge in awareness has resulted from Daniel Goleman's synthesized work, resulting in the popularization of emotion through the term 'emotional intelligence'.

In general, this has characterized a resurgence of interest in the powerful concept of emotion in educational practice, and the concepts of 'emotional literacy', 'emotional competence', 'critical emotional literacy', 'emotional intelligence' and 'socio-emotional learning' are all part of the emotional vocabulary used in education today.

But what are emotions? Emotions are unlearned reactions that are pre-wired into our brains as part of evolutionary survival mechanisms that are elaborated and reinforced by our cultures and laws. They are, however, adjustable and adaptable, but most importantly learners need to understand how their emotions influence their thinking and behaviour on a daily basis. Children (and adults) also need to be able to critique their emotions, identifying how they are manipulated in the made world including social, political and cultural contexts, as well as needing to understand the implication of their emotionally informed decisions on other people's emotions.

Feelings or emotions?

When discussing emotions we tend to use the terms 'emotion' and 'feelings' interchangeably, as clearly there is an association. Generally it is considered that there is a set of basic emotions in all cultures: happiness, sadness, surprise, disgust, anger and fear. These emotions are our primary responses; they are built into our DNA and are chemical neurobiological responses.

Feelings can, however, be considered as the residue of our emotions. They are part of our conscious warning system. When we reflect upon an event it is likely that we can associate with the feelings more so than with the emotion, as feelings are a subset of all of our mind-body states (such as disappointment, hunger, hope and so on). There are hundreds of these different feelings and culturally we react with different feelings to different emotions in different environments. Therefore, feelings are partly a learned and reinforced response in the culture in which you grow up (the family, the peers, the community and so on) and become the warning system for the emotion that stops us from attempting to revisit that emotion.

Essentially, emotions are subconscious directors of our attention that occur prior to our feelings. They are the drivers of our cognitive and physiological attention and are ultimately complex, primitive and difficult to define, yet they provide a reflexive ordinance system that influences our behaviour, decision making and creative thinking.

> 'Anyone can become angry. That is easy. But to be angry with the right person, to the right degree, at the right time, for the right purpose and in the right way – that is not easy.'
>
> Aristotle

And finally . . .

This book is about helping students and teachers. However, caution is required. The emotions are complex and in terms of psychology many teachers are entering this area for the first time. This book is an introduction to the topic to build upon good practice. Teachers should therefore proceed with caution and students must be given the chance to opt out of activities that they feel uncomfortable participating in.

The teacher and emotion

What is emotional literacy?

Generally emotional literacy is an educational term, as opposed to emotional intelligence, which tends to be used by industry and businesses. There are many definitions but generally it is considered as our ability through thinking to recognize, manage, comprehend and suitably communicate our emotions and to understand how they shape our actions and relationships and influence our thinking.

Within education, and including the *Every Child Matters* agenda, emotional literacy can be considered to involve a range of agencies interested in the well-being of children. Within this context emotional literacy is unlikely to be a single timetabled slot activity but is part of a coordinated and synergized activity that has a clearly managed strategy, linking with the Every Child Matters Agenda, which might include: promotion of health (including mental health), learning (including behaviour for learning), citizenship, social, spiritual, cultural and moral activities, equal opportunities and personal development.

The reality is that the emotional space of life has been relegated to one of inconvenience in a fast-paced world. It is therefore important that all teachers have an awareness of emotional literacy and a willingness to consider its position within their daily life, whether this is through the curriculum or through pastoral or managerial roles that they undertake.

Finally, a misconception that is worth challenging early on is that emotional literacy is only for those children who we perceive as vulnerable and at risk. While these children may be the priority in terms of our attention, ultimately all children require the ability to untangle their emotions to better understand their daily actions and interactions.

Advice

It is important that all teachers recognize the powerful influence of emotions, both on themselves and on the learning environment. By recognizing the significance of emotions, teachers become empowered as they are able to unravel some of the complexities of the classroom.

Using emotional literacy

Read through the list below as it is important to decide how you most want to use this book. Knowing what you want at the start means you are more likely to find what you want. You may need to read a bit more if you are unfamiliar with the topic. However, when you have read more, come back and reflect on some of the possible ways that you might consider developing emotional literacy in your learning environment.

Possible ways of using this book	Yes	No	Maybe
To use as an introduction to the topic for yourself and follow up the further reading section.			
To use a page as the basis of a discussion in each of your staff meetings across the year.			
To use the book as a focus of an INSET day.			
To use selected activities with children in lessons.			
To use as part of developing a policy on emotional literacy.			
To split the book up across different subjects and years as part of a mapping exercise for emotional literacy across the school.			
To use as the basis of future assemblies.			
To use snippets to send to parents in newsletters as part of their education about emotional literacy.			

Application

The Neanderthal in the classroom

Are you the kind of teacher that lights up children's faces when you walk into the classroom? Or are you the kind of teacher that when you leave the classroom, children's faces light up!

If it was pointed out to you that your classroom was full of Neanderthals you might think, 'Too right it is, particularly on a wet and windy Friday afternoon!' If, however, you as the teacher were included in that list of Neanderthals in the classroom, then you might be less inclined to agree.

The reality is that our bodies and emotions have not changed significantly for about 30,000 years and while society, technology and civilization has moved on, our brains are still predominantly operating in the same way. This can lead to some conflict. The classic example is our dependency upon fat and sugar, which is pre-wired into our brains to ensure we can keep warm and have enough energy to walk long distances. Such requirements are no longer a requirement in a society of cars and central heating, even though we are still pre-programmed to gorge on these foods, which are now readily available. As a consequence we tend to overeat, exploited by junk food manufacturers who take advantage of this weakness in our brains. Such emotionally outdated conflicts are called the Savanna principle. There are many such principles that govern our daily life but which are long outdated.

A further example of the Savanna principle can include environmental threat. For instance we have an innate fear of fire, but interestingly not of smoking; of spiders, but not skin cancer. This is because these genuine threats to existence were not a threat 30,000 years ago and are relatively modern. Equally we innately fear tigers, spiders and snakes far more than we do cars, even though cars on a daily basis pose a far greater threat than any animal.

Such potentially irrational emotions influence our thinking, yet as they are the only emotions we have we tend to simply accept and get on with them. However, emotional literacy offers us all the space to reconsider how our emotions sometimes mislead us.

Advice

Discussing fears

Discuss innate fears with your group to see how we often have disproportionate and outdated fears. Ask them to rank their fears. These fears are not to be overlooked but they are a good way of showing how our emotions automatically influence how we feel.

- terrorist attack
- bitten by a snake
- car accident
- DIY
- murder by a stranger.

Then discuss in the context of the information below, explaining how such fears are both innate and cultured by folklore and the media.

Terrorist attack	Although terrorist attacks are a real fear the number of victims of terrorism is tiny compared to car accidents, DIY and food poisoning.
Bitten by a snake	Only around six to ten people die each year from bites of all snake species in the USA. The figure in the UK is negligible.
Car accident	Every year 1,500 car drivers and adult passengers die in road accidents and 1,000 pedestrians and cyclists are killed and 40,000 are injured. Each year in England nearly 180 children die and almost 4,800 are injured as pedestrians or cyclists.
DIY	In 1999 national statistics indicated that there were 200,000 DIY injuries in the UK and 70 deaths – far more than any terrorist attack.
Murder by a stranger	The percentage of people murdered by a complete stranger is tiny. Although we automatically are wired to fear strangers we are more likely to be attacked by someone we know than by someone we don't know.

Application

Progression and emotional awareness

There are many different types of emotion that are referred to in the literature. However a useful hierarchy of emotion has been created by McPhail, which can be used for teachers to consider the concept of progression in terms of the development of learners' emotional capabilities. McPhail considers emotions as being central to an individual's ability to establish which problems they should solve and in which order they should address them, being aware that emotions act as a filter that directs our attention, becoming a reflexive ordinance system.

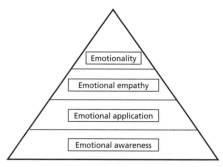

McPhail's level of emotional awareness

If we consider the top two tiers of McPhail's levels of emotional awareness, then I would suggest emotional empathy and emotionality are at the very heart of what we are attempting to do in education. That is, first, nurture emotional empathy, as in the ability to understand others people's emotions and how we impact upon them with our decision making and through the action we take.

Second, emotionality represents being aware of our emotions and how they guide our decision-making processes. Such emotional capabilities are consistent with definitions of emotional literacy, such as the ability to recognize, understand and express your emotions, helping yourself and others to succeed.

Finally, emotional awareness is recognizing and identifying your own and others' emotions, while emotional application is recognizing how you use your emotions and how others use their emotions on you.

Advice

Progression in emotional literacy

In each box write down in what forms you might be delivering these areas of emotional capability. Consider if they are to be delivered in a progressive way or random manner. If random, you may need to consider how the different levels of emotionality are scaffolded.

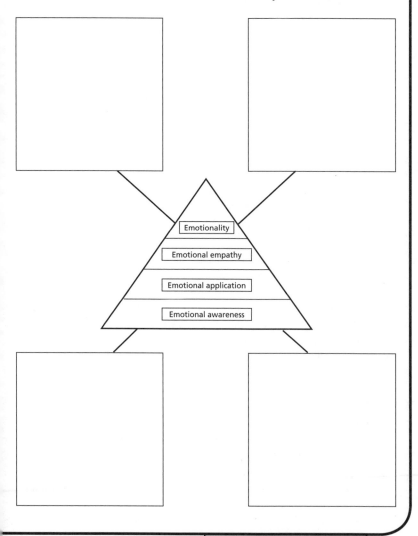

Emotionality

Emotional empathy

Emotional application

Emotional awareness

Fight or flight

Have you ever been in a situation where you just don't seem to be capable of thinking in your usual way, where your thinking appears irrational and overly biased to one particular outcome?

Most will be able to locate the amygdala as the controlling part of the brain in this situation. This part of the brain is referred to as the storehouse of the reptilian 'old brain' with innate memory as its early warning system preparing the body to respond, often without thinking, to a particular threat. Popular psychology calls this the 'fight or flight' scenario, where fight represents our response using aggressive, combative behaviour, while flight represents fleeing a scene using multiple senses to escape a perceived predator. Although extreme environments will demand such responsive behaviour even mildly threatening environments, common in many classrooms, can provoke similar responses where we are unable to think straight as our amygdala is taking control. It is calculated that it takes around seven milliseconds for these warning signals to transmit to the thalamus and a few milliseconds further for the thalamus to relay them to the amygdala. To which the adage is best described as 'I feel before I think'.

Daniel Goleman has described this as 'hijacking of the amygdala', as the thalamus quickly reacts to potential threats and so distracts the conscious rational part of our brain. In such cases it bypasses the cortex, the conscious processing part of the brain, and sends the signal straight to the amygdala, which reacts based on previously stored patterns. On such occasions the body shuts down a whole range of functions such as hair growth and saliva production (hence dry mouth) to focus its attention on that one event that will increase the chances of survival.

Within the learning environment this is happening continually, as the brain is constantly reacting to potential perceived threats that will distract the brain for learning. The reality is we are often reacting without fully having time to cognate or see what we are reacting to and the challenge is therefore to create an effective learning environment based upon a high challenge and low stress environment.

Advice

Strategies to avoid fight or flight

Identify possible fight or flight scenarios in your classroom and think about how you can reduce the stress in these situations. Think about the scenarios below on the left and how you might try and overcome some of the potentially stressful situations. You might need to read some of the other sections, particularly communicating (Chapter 3), before you can complete the table.

Scenario	Strategies to avoid fight or flight
Students entry into the room	For example, control entry, adopt routines, smile and welcome.
Taking of register	
Collecting in homework	
Question and answer	
Room temperature	
Difficult concepts to learn	
Low level disruption	
Student exit	
Wet break	
Other	

Application

Recognizing your own emotions

There is a story about a teacher who goes to see the headteacher to offer her resignation as the children in her class are completely out of control. Unfortunately he has to deal with another problem at that time so asks her to wait in his office.

While in his office waiting she sees on the headteacher's desk her class list with some numbers next to her pupils' names, with particularly high numbers next to some of her most naughty pupils. She starts to think perhaps little William with a score of 147 isn't that naughty after all. Jabir has a score of 143 while Shirley, who has been causing lots of problems, must just be over exuberant as she has a score of 150.

When the headteacher returns, the teacher tells him it didn't matter and goes back to her class. A few days later the headteacher pops into her classroom and notices a much more relaxed atmosphere, with the teacher appearing to be relaxed and the children seeming to be engaged and enjoying the lesson.

'Glad to see you have sorted things out,' he says 'and by the way here is your class list with your children's new locker key numbers on.'

If only it were true!

The point is, do you stop and think about how your emotions influence how you feel and what you see? The reality is our emotions constantly react subconsciously to a whole series of events with decreasing levels of sensitivity, producing a sense of indifference and apathy. It is therefore essential that adults and children recognize the extent to which they become desensitized to a whole range of issues and try to regain some emotional balance.

While disassociation of our emotions may essentially help some people (such as doctors and even teachers) through the day, it is important that we reframe our thinking through a process of association of what is really happening.

Sometimes, however, we get the balance of our emotions wrong. For instance, by only associating positively with events you may feel completely great but may ultimately not be in touch with reality. Equally, by constantly dissociating with negative events you may feel great. However you may again not be engaging with reality.

Advice

Association/disassociation

Collect a series of images from a newspaper or magazine that portray newsworthy events or take a topic from your curriculum area that has implications upon people's lives. Ask groups of students to take on one of the association or disassociation dispositions (from 1–4) and complete what someone with that character would take from such an experience or event.

1	Association with positive experience (always focuses on the positive).	3	Disassociation with negative experience (always ignores the negative).
2	Association with negative experience (always focuses on the negative).	4	Disassociation with positive experience (always ignores the positive).

Get students to feed back and discuss the different dispositions. The point of the exercise being to recognize that we are not likely to be extremes of the above, but that we each might often take up a stance of association and disassociation to a series of events on a daily basis without knowing it.

Dealing with sensitive issues

'Don't cry because it's over. Smile because it happened.'

Dr Seuss

One of the fears that teachers may have when dealing with emotional issues in the school environment is that they may have difficulty dealing with sensitive and emotional issues that they feel uncomfortable with. Within this context it is important that teachers acknowledge that they may sometimes also be vulnerable and they have to know the correct lines of responsibility for coping with such matters, particularly when dealing with potential child protection issues.

However, a key part of emotional literacy is recognizing our own concerns, as well as educating students as to how to be able to deal with sensitive issues in more effective ways. Such sensitive issues may include:

- relationships
- substance and alcohol abuse
- sexuality
- politics and religion
- lifestyles and values
- environmental issues.

While it is recognized that teachers may have their own opinions on these, it is not the role of teachers to express or promote their own particular preferences. In addition, going into areas that we are ill equipped to advise upon or where the teacher has overly strong feelings can actually do more harm than good. It is therefore important to recognize and value children's rights and to abide by their decision not to share what may be sensitive issues with adults or other children.

Building trust in an environment is, however, an important and essential part of emotional development and through such difficult and sensitive contexts students can significantly learn an important range of skills, which includes listening to others, recognizing other points of view, managing conflict, arguing a case and dealing with recognizing their own feelings and those of others.

Advice

Dealing with personal issues

All teachers need to be aware of and prepared to handle personal issues arising from discussion work, which may involve sensitive issues. In order to do so, consider the following and ask whether there is clear guidance:

- Who is responsible for child protection issues?
- What represents overly sensitive issues that should be addressed in more appropriate settings?
- Is there a classroom environment in which students can express a point of view without fear that they may differ from those held either by staff or their peers?
- How do classes behave towards each other when expressing contrary views?
- Are the differences between individuals valued and celebrated?
- Are you able to listen to and learn from the experiences of others, showing sensitivity?
- Are parents informed when particularly sensitive issues may be discussed and how can they help in extending their child's emotional literacy capability?
- Do students have access to balanced information and differing views with which they ensure they take due care of the needs of individual's social, cultural or personal identity?

It is important in such circumstances that all staff are aware that they are not able to offer students or their parents unconditional confidentiality. Any member of staff who receives information about behaviour that is likely to cause harm to the child or to others must pass it on to the appropriate agency following the school's child protection procedures.

Application

Emotion in the staffroom

'I've learned that people will forget what you said, people will forget what you did, but people will never forget how you made them feel.'

Maya Angelou

Teaching has consistently been ranked as an emotionally stressful occupation, with around 40 per cent of teachers frequently reporting being very or extremely stressed as a result of factors intrinsic to their work. Part of this can be ascribed to association and disassociation (see Recognizing your own emotions, page 12) of our emotions at the wrong times through not recognizing what is and isn't in the teacher's control.

The most frequently reported factors causing stress include students' disruptive behaviour, workload, school ethos and lack of support from colleagues and/or managers. As such, the levels of distress among teachers has been found to be twice that of the general population. When compared with the psychological health of 26 different professions, teaching was found to be one of the six most stressful occupations. Differences have also been found between the stress levels of male and female teachers, with female teachers consistently scoring higher on measures of anxiety, distress and depression.

It is also known that stress is translated into the classroom and is manifest through our emotions by overreacting, creating a vicious circle and so increasing teacher and student stress, leading to an escalation of problems.

The solutions are not easy but it is worth remembering that the fight or flight syndrome applies to teachers also. Therefore, if you do have anxiety, it is likely that you will not be able to think clearly in such situations and will need to adopt some anxiety reducing measures.

Advice

What, when, how, why?

Recognize your own emotions by identifying 'what', 'when', 'how' and 'why' causes of stress. Use the table to identity what is in your control and not in your control and whether you are recognizing your own emotions by overly associating or disassociating (see page 13). When doing this try to be specific, so it won't be all your colleagues and students all of the time. It may only be a few students or colleagues at occasional times that cause your anxiety.

What causes me stress?	When does it cause me stress?	How does it cause me stress?	Why does it cause me stress?	What can I do?

Laughter: the best medicine

A snail got mugged by two tortoises. When he went to the police, they questioned him as to what happened. He said, 'I don't know, it all happened so fast!'

As mentioned in the introduction to this book, emotions have suffered something of a bad press recently, as we tend to view them negatively. Yet there is no finer sound than a group of children laughing and we know there are a whole range of benefits to laughter, including:

- immunity system increases
- suppresses stress related hormones
- stimulates production of serotonin
- increases cardiovascular activity
- increases oxygen intake
- lowers blood pressure
- improves mood
- increases brain functioning
- develops instant relaxation
- exercises muscle groups.

Also, in one research experiment, children were shown a five-minute comedy clip prior to a creativity exercise and it was found to have a significant positive effect on their performance.

Joke telling ultimately involves complex verbal and visual associations and timing, as well as managing and manipulating a range of emotions – so give it a go.

That reminds me. I went to see the doctor and he said 'Lie down on the couch.' I said, 'Are you going to examine me?' and he said 'No, I am going to clean the floor!'

Knock knock
Who's there?
Please hold! Your knock is important to me. Your knock will be answered in the order it was knocked.

Advice

Tell a joke

Evolutionary psychology tells us that laughing is the primitive response of releasing tension manifested in the relief from fear of what might have happened. So tell a joke to your class, ask them what they find funny, explain what's going on when we laugh at the wrong time and how laughing makes us feel better. This is the only emotional joke I know – of which there are other varieties!

A couple decided to have a party and invited lots of people, telling them to bring their friends. On the invitation it read: Themed Party – Come As A Human Emotion.

The first guest arrives and the couple open the door to see a woman covered in green paint with the letters N and V painted on her chest. 'Wow, great outfit, what emotion have you come as?' and the woman says, 'I'm green with envy.' The couple reply, 'Brilliant, come on in and have a drink.'

Later the next guest arrives and the host opens the door to see a man covered in a pink body stocking with a feather boa wrapped round his most intimate parts. 'Wow, great outfit, what emotion have you come as?' He replies, 'I'm tickled pink.' The host says, 'Fantastic, come on in and join the party.'

A few minutes later the doorbell goes for the third time and the host opens the door to see two men, one standing naked in a bowl of custard and the other dressed as a pear. The host is really shocked and says, 'Guys what you have done? You could get arrested for standing like that out there. What emotion is this supposed to be?' The first man replies, 'Well, I'm "discustard" and my friend is here as "despair"!'

Emotion: a different kind of intelligence

'Let's not forget that the little emotions are the great captains of our lives and we obey them without realising it.'

Vincent Van Gogh (1889)

Howard Gardner wrote *Frames of Mind* (1983) in which he created a list of multiple intelligences that changed the way we think about intelligence, particularly the way we perceive the logical and the mathematical as the key intelligences. In his list of intelligences, although focusing more on cognition than feelings, two of them (interpersonal and intrapersonal) are directly related to emotion and feelings and it is argued that these forms of intelligence are essential to our development and well-being and that certain individuals exemplify these forms of intelligence.

Daniel Goleman followed this with *Emotional Intelligence* (1996), in which he lists five important features of emotional intelligence:

- self-awareness (knowing your emotions)
- mood management (handling feelings)
- self-motivation ('gathering up' your feelings and directing yourself towards a goal)
- empathy (recognizing feelings in others)
- managing relationships (handling interpersonal interaction).

Just over ten years after *Frames of Mind* was written, Antonio Damasio rocked the 'intelligence-measurers' boat again with his book, *Descartes' Error* (1995) where he reinforced that one's emotional life is a primitive brain function left over from our evolutionary history, which represents the core capacity for all human reason.

We therefore need to recognize that our emotions are primarily primitive and reflexive. By recognizing our own emotions, and those of others, through the concept of emotional literacy therefore develops a different kind of intelligence.

Advice

Think about your class in different ways

Although it is tempting to regard all students by their academic capabilities, think about how you can value different emotional capabilities and how you can share how you value these different emotional capabilities.

Students who are loyal to their friends.	Students who are good at managing relationships.	Students who are good at managing their feelings.	Students who are open with their feelings.	Students who are good at sensing the mood of the class and lifting spirits.

Emotional ambivalence

One of my fears for children is the concept of emotional ambivalence and the notion that they may become desensitized to some of their emotions. For example, it is calculated that the number of murders seen on television by the time an average child reaches 14 years old is around 8,000, while the number of violent acts seen on television by the age of 18 is approximately 200,000. The number of 30-second television commercials seen in a year by an average child is 20,000. While considering these figures it is also important to remember that these are not just casual engagements with ad hoc material. This material is precise and calculated and powerfully driven to have a maximum emotional impact upon the viewer. Such modern day bombardment with images, sounds and products creates a constant search for stimulation and distraction to prevent the 'quieting of our minds', thus not allowing reflection, and as a consequence the emotional 'space' in our life is often resigned to that of an inconvenience in the fast-paced modern life.

Beyond school, the concept of emotional development is made all the more urgent by what has been described as the post-emotional society, which results in pre-packaged, manufactured emotions – a 'happy meal' or the 'McDonaldization of emotions consumed by the masses'. In effect we are told how we should be emotional, which in today's post-emotional society the response is ambivalence and intellectual rationalization, creating a lack of engagement and often a superficial and materialistic existence.

A day without emotion

Get your group to consider a day without emotion from the moment they wake up, focusing on several key issues such as relationships, school life and so on. Most importantly get them to list both the emotions and the difficulties that you would have if you didn't have that emotion. Some possible starting points are:

- Interacting with people. Imagine not caring about other people's emotions or feelings or even your own. What would a conversation be like?

- Daily activities such as getting to school. Imagine if you had no fear. What would be your chances of getting to school successfully?

- Imagine certain careers. What would it be like to not have any emotions?

- Entertainment – imagine television or radio devoid of emotion.

Locating emotion

'Whatever we plant in our subconscious mind and nourish with repetition and emotion will one day become a reality.'

Earl Nightingale

Our emotions are often inseparable from our physiological state. For example, we often get an increased heart rate when excited or 'butterflies' in the tummy when anxious and as such we traditionally associate feelings with parts of our body rather than with the 2 kg of cells known as the brain. Traditionally, it was also thought that such emotions were processed consciously and then referred for an affective reaction with the belief being that we decide what we think, and then we subconsciously decide how we feel about it. Damasio, in his *Descartes' Error*, states, however, that the real order of things is likely to be the opposite of this, as he suggests that the subconscious processing in our brain is a reaction to our feelings, therefore making us think about it. Thus, what we feel about something may inform us what we think rather than the other way round. Such understanding makes the term 'thinking about it made me feel . . .' slightly redundant, as actually feeling it made you think about it. It is also worth considering the attachment and additional value that is given to everyday emotive language such as 'speaking from the heart', 'my gut feeling is' or 'I felt touched by'.

So the current state of thinking related to our emotions are that those physiological feelings that we have are happening subconsciously before they are then referred to our conscious thinking. This means that the feelings may not always be rational and we should be critical of these feelings as they may not always be our best guide.

Advice

This chapter discusses some of the issues related to the brain, teaching, learning and emotion.

The brain is a wonderful organ. It starts working the moment you get up in the morning and does not stop until you get into school!

Language and emotion

With your class, think about how our everyday language may use emotion and discuss where and why we may use these terms.

Term	Where	Why
1 For example, 'Speaking from the heart . . .'	When trying to persuade someone.	Suggests that this is not something that is thought about but it is something that you care about.
2 For example, 'My gut feeling is . . .'		
3 For example, 'I felt so . . .'		
4 For example, 'How would you feel if . . .?'		
5		
6		
7		
8		
9		
10		

Application

Teachers thinking about emotion

Comfort the disturbed – disturb the comfortable.

One of the difficulties with discussing emotion as a topic in education is that it can often be perceived in very narrow terms. This means that teachers may think that discussions are not relevant for them as emotion is only for the vulnerable and needy.

A much more sophisticated view is recognizing a differentiated approach to dealing with emotion and recognizing that the teacher's role is a variable one where you are dealing with two extremes.

First, sometimes your role is a comforting one where you are helping the needy, insecure and the vulnerable by providing a sense of security. This might be through reassuring them in the curriculum or pastoral side of your work.

Alternatively, your role may at times be one where you are deliberately targeting learner's emotions to make them feel uncertain or unsure (see Pedagogy of discomfort, page 98). This is where you might be challenging misconceptions that learners may have or where you are being deliberately provocative so that the students can explore different and challenging emotions such as uncertainty and anxiety.

The role of the teacher is therefore a complex one as getting this the right way round and the various phases in between correct is both difficult and complex, as well as requiring confidence, experience and expertise.

It is important to note that the teacher should not be considering emotion as a 'secret garden'. Instead, it is essential that emotion should be considered and discussed as part of developing learner's emotional literacy and as such it involves getting them to reflect on their emotions, as well as those emotions modelled by the teacher.

Advice

Emotional planning

This activity helps you think about the emotional aspects of your teaching in further detail. Think briefly about the emotions/feelings you may be employing during your teaching week and complete the timetable below. For instance, if you are teaching a Year 11 class on Friday afternoon who may be anxious about examinations, you may plan to emotionally reassure them. Equally you might be dealing with a potentially dry topic on Wednesday, lesson 1, where you will need to emotionally engage the learners.

If for some lessons it is difficult to anticipate how you will be relating to learner's emotions before the event, you can equally do this activity in retrospect. Most importantly you will begin to realize the extent that emotions play a part in all aspects of school life.

	Lesson 1	Lesson 2	Lesson 3	Lesson 4	Lesson 5
Monday					
Tuesday					
Wednesday					
Thursday					
Friday					

Application

We feel therefore we learn

The teacher, after discussing how Hitler killed over six million people, asked: 'Now class, after what I have told you – how do you feel?'

Response from student: 'Miss, he never did nothing to me.'

Although potentially amusing, such a misconception reveals how dispassionate we can all become, particularly if we cannot see the relevance to something and how it impacts upon our own lives or that of others. Such disassociation has been called a 'McDonaldization of our emotions', where they become pre-packaged and distanced from the true experience. Whether it be a holocaust, earthquake or tsunami, it is easy to convince ourselves that it has 'little to do with me'.

With children this is compounded with brain changes around the ages of 10–18, when increasing amounts of dopamine creates the effect of learners appearing almost intoxicated in their thinking. The amount of dopamine is controlled by the brain's emotional system, and while dopamine makes us feel good the behaviour that might accompany dopamine production may not be. As has been suggested our emotional brain wants to spend out the credit card, even though our logical brain knows we should save for a rainy day. Added to this are the other physical and social changes that come with puberty, and it becomes apparent that the learner's interest lies predominantly with themselves.

Therefore (not that teachers didn't already know this) teaching and learning becomes even more difficult in the teenage years. The teacher's role is to try to navigate a route between the learner's emotional engagement and the topic they are wanting to deliver, using stories and metaphors and strong contexts so that learners can be placed in a situation where they really can imagine how they would feel within the context of the topic. Such emotional engagement is central to good leaning and motivation and without it learning becomes too abstract, leading to emotional disconnection.

Advice

Creative writing

'First they came for the Communists but I was not a
Communist, so I did not speak out;
Then they came for the Socialists and the Trade Unionists but I
was not one of them, so I did not speak out;
Then they came for the Jews but I was not Jewish, so I did not
speak out.
And when they came for me, there was no one left to speak
out for me.'

Martin Niemoller (1892–1984)

The above is a well-known poem about disassociation and can be
used as a useful exercise for almost any topic as a basis for engaging
learners in their learning.

In groups, learners can take a topic (for example, sustainability, local
planning, food additives, environmental issues and so on) they are
working on and think about the wider impact of the topic and the
wider interests groups for the topic. Then they can use the structure of
the topic to structure their own emotional, creative writing exercise.

Emotion and decision making

'When dealing with people, remember you are not dealing with creatures of logic, but creatures of emotion.'

Dale Carnegie

Most of us will, by way of popular psychology, be familiar with the 'fight or flight' scenario and will be able to locate the amygdala as the controlling part of the brain in this situation. To which the adage is best described as 'I feel before I think'.

This brain is said to have evolved from the bottom up and the amygdala is located near the base of the brain and tends to be referred to as the storehouse of 'old brain'/innate memory, as its early warning system prepares the body to respond. It takes less than a blink of an eye, about seven milliseconds, for these warning signals to transmit to the thalamus, and a few milliseconds more for the thalamus to relay them to the amygdala.

The truth is we are often reacting without fully having time to cognate or see what we are reacting to. Have you ever opened a cupboard and caught something falling out without ever really seeing it? Ever done it the dark? The reality is that we are reacting all the time and if we were ever able to compute all the senses that we have managed to suppress then our mind's thinking would collapse under the sheer mass of information.

With children the tendency is to rely even more heavily on their emotions, as they often don't know how to react in a variety of cases. So often when frightened or intimidated they will tend to 'lash out' (fight) rather than standing back and reflecting.

Stress, anxiety, punishments, rewards and strong emotions all play a part in reducing the flexibility of our thinking, potentially leading to irrational behaviour and influencing our decision making.

Reflecting upon decision making allows all adults and children the opportunity to identify how their decisions may be overly influenced by their emotions and allows us to critique our emotions – essential features of emotional literacy.

Advice

Fight or flight lesson

The key to this lesson is to draw on the differences between positive and negative emotions, how we might deal with these emotions and how they might overly influence our thinking, e.g. 'fight or flight'.

For this lesson you will need some materials for learners to make posters.

Lesson outline:

First, discuss with learners their definition of stressful situations. Record these on a whiteboard and discuss as a group any commonalities between the situations. A key point is that stress is a very powerful feeling that may make us react in certain ways. Get learners to list on their posters what stress does to them. Record these ideas on a whiteboard, then discuss some of the bodily changes that happen with stress, which might include crying, heart racing, temperature rising and so on.

Introduce the concept of 'fight or flight', highlighting that many of the feelings that we have in stressful situations are perfectly natural but that we need to be aware of these feelings changing our thinking.

Next, put the learners into groups and get them to produce a poster for the group that has one of the following displayed at the top:

- group 1 – things that make me feel sad
- group 2 – things that make me feel happy
- group 3 – things that make me feel angry
- group 4 – things that make me feel worried
- group 5 – things that make me feel frustrated
- group 6 – things that I feel I don't want to happen.

Each group then has a couple of minutes to record their responses to the feeling at the top of their poster. After a couple of minutes the group moves to the next poster and does the same.

When the group finally arrives back at their own poster get them to discuss any similarities that they can group together. Finally get one person from each group to feed back from their group and then discuss issues, similarities and so on.

Application

When our emotions take the lead

'Any emotion, if it is sincere, is involuntary.'

Mark Twain

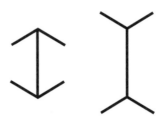

Mueller-Lyre illusion

The above is a well-known illusion called the Mueller-Lyre illusion where we have two lines (the central lines) exactly the same length, yet when we look at them we actually see the line on the right looking longer. So what? The point is that something in our brain is subconsciously adjusting the way we see the lines and adjusting what we think. Interestingly, people brought up in more natural environments than industrial landscapes don't always see the illusion. The point therefore is that although this happens with our visual system, the same is also happening with our emotional system. Often we are feeling something that has become subconsciously distorted.

This is known as the rational/emotional dualism and is a defective emotional response similar to irrational phobias, which although we recognize them to have little foundation (just as above we know the lines are the same length) result from peculiarities or damage to specific emotional systems. For example 'hippopotomonstrosesquippedaliophobia' is a persistent, abnormal and unwarranted fear of long words, while 'phobophobia' is a fear of phobias! The reality is although our phobias may be apparent to us while also recognized as irrational, our subconscious emotional irrationalities may not always be quite so obvious unless we take time to reflect on how our emotions influence our thinking and decision making.

Advice

Are you sure?

This is an activity that can be done with most students and even by yourself. Have you ever done something that you regretted, jumped to the wrong conclusion or got the wrong idea, yet when thinking about it dispassionately would you have followed a different line of thinking? One way at looking at situations is to use the TRUTH table below to help you come up with more rationale thoughts by reflecting upon past, bad and emotionally led decisions.

Trigger	What happened . . .?
Reference	What did you incorrectly think . . .?
Unusual response	What did you say or do that was wrong . . .?
Truth	What were the true events . . .?
Healthy response	What should you have done and what should you do next time . . .?

Application

Fooling the brain

'Children are the living messages we send to a time we will not see.'

John W. Whitehead

Shakespeare pointed out that we go to the theatre to be fooled and when we think about our brains we are constantly being fooled on a daily basis. Think about our watching of television. Research has shown that when watching our favourite television programs our brains create the same chemicals as when we are sat talking to friends. Therefore, although we know the characters are not real, we still benefit in the same way we would when with friends.

Think also about magic. If you know anything about magic, you know it is just about fooling someone's brain and emotions. It is making someone focus on an illusion that we know does not exist.

Perhaps the most bizarre of all is ventriloquism, which although we know it makes absolutely no sense, it somehow engages the brain. While all this makes life fun and entertaining, it also makes getting a sense of reality difficult.

A large part of emotional literacy is understanding this fooling the brain. It is adding rationality to an often irrational emotional process. Therefore, we often don't see or feel things as *they* are but rather we see and feel things as *we* are. The world is not as it seems. We see what we see as reality in a highly filtered and distorted reality. Therefore, the key is to understand ourselves better and recognize the flaws in our intuitive emotional systems.

Understanding reality, however, might not be so simple. For instance, my 8-year-old son and I can both watch the same film but see very different stories and have very different experiences, even though we both enjoy it. Therefore, an essential part of this is discussion and respect for the opinions of others, and mutual realities, without viewing one person's reality better than another.

Advice

Believing what you see

We believe whatever we see or feel to represent our view of reality, yet we all have a slightly different and distorted view based upon our past experiences. As such we tend to view various scenarios in different ways.

For example, have you ever been looking at a problem in such a complex way that you rejected the simple solutions without thinking about them? The reality is that some things in life are far more complex than they appear, while some things are simpler than they appear. If we merely rely on our emotions and past experience to guide us, then we may be missing the elephant in the room. Therefore, we need to understand ourselves much more before we can begin to see we all lead a partially blinkered experience.

To demonstrate this, visit: www.viscog.beckman.uiuc.edu/grafs/demos/15.html.

When you watch the video you need to count the number of times the white team passes the ball – you have one go only at this.

Do not read on until you have done this.

OK, if you are reading this you have either done the experiment or you are not doing the experiment. If you have not watched the video for a second time, do so without counting the passes and see if you notice anything different.

If you are anything like the vast majority of people you will be shocked to see something walking across the screen on the second occasion that you didn't notice the first time. If not convinced, show your class and see how many don't notice anything. The reality is that this is an excellent metaphor for illustrating that all the time events are going on unnoticed and we are often only receiving a limited and selective view of what we perceive reality to be.

Application

3

Communicating

Communicating our feelings

'I have heard there are troubles of more than one kind.
Some come from ahead and some come from behind.
But I've bought a big bat.
I'm all ready you see.
Now my troubles are going to have troubles with me!'

Dr Seuss

In the English language we have around 3,000 words that help us locate, identify and express our feelings. An interesting exercise is to examine the extent that you as a teacher may have a sophisticated emotional vocabulary and also the extent to which you use this in your daily activities.

Part of this is extending children's emotional vocabulary, as it is generally recognized that children who have a wider vocabulary are able to locate their emotions and feelings more effectively and as a consequence are happier. To develop this ability to communicate they have to regularly engage and critique literature, performances, media and products so that they can recognize how their emotions are engaged, challenged and manipulated by the different emotions.

How emotions and language work together is not fully understood. However, it appears that by naming a feeling we help our subconscious processing access the emotional part of the brain where feelings are located. This is central to emotional literacy and therefore the more opportunities that teachers build in activities, in all subjects, to locate the emotional vocabulary associated with an activity, the more emotionally literate the learners will become.

Advice

Central to developing emotional literacy is the ability to communicate and express our feelings effectively, while also being able to recognize the emotions and feelings of others. As with any literacy, extending the vocabulary of feelings is essential to this.

Emotional language

There are two parts to this activity.

The first part is to consider the location of emotional language in your daily teaching. So the first question is, do you have a rich and declarative emotional language?

There are several ways to do this. First, just by being more aware and making a note of the amount of times you use emotional language in your teaching.

Second, you may want to formalize this by recording your voice during a lesson and then listening out for and noting your emotional vocabulary.

Finally, as part of a peer review or coaching activity you might want to ask for the focus to be on the extent that you engage learners using your emotional vocabulary in your lesson. This might also include considering how often you ask students to try to identify an emotion/feeling (for example, 'How would you feel if . . .?'), which again can be formalized using the above processes.

Application

Non-verbal communication

'Feelings are 55% body language, 38% tone and 7% words.'

Albert Mehrabian

Without opening our mouths we are already communicating with each other in a whole variety of ways, with research indicating that up to 90 per cent of our communication is non-verbal. A huge percentage of what our brain perceives in communication from others is focused (subconsciously) on non-verbal signals such as eye movements, facial gestures, hand gestures, tone of voice or head movements. In fact, the whole silent movie era depended upon conveying such information non-verbally. Therefore, the way we walk, stand and look is sending out a whole set of signals, including our emotions, that can be read. So as one part of the brain is processing the words while talking, other parts are continually focusing on and responding to the non-verbal communication that accompanies the words. When observing a teacher, students can literally sense a whole range of emotions such as their interest and enthusiasm.

It has, however, been shown that boys and certain special needs children such as those on the autistic spectrum are unable to, or are particularly poor at, reading body language and facial expressions. As a result they are only getting a reduced version of what is being communicated – often resulting in mixed messages. In developing emotional literacy it is therefore important that we recognize this, as well as developing an understanding of how people convey emotions non-verbally as part of children's emotional development.

Role play, as well as asking questions such as those below about non-verbal communication, can also begin to increase learners' understanding of the significance of non-verbal communications.

- When someone is speaking to you, should you look at them?
- How should you look and stand to show someone you are interested in what they are saying?
- How can you tell if someone isn't really interested when talking?
- When someone walks past you (such as a neighbour) do you know how you should respond?
- How can you tell by looking if someone is sad or unhappy?

Advice

Identifying non-verbal communication

This is an activity that can be discussed with students. (See also Appendix 1)

There are said to be main body postures for communicating non-verbally (of course there are many subtle variations). Using a video of people doing everyday activities, see if you can identify any of the following five (or combinations of) body postures for non-verbal communication:

● Computing/thinking – when someone seems to be hiding emotions by being deep in thought. The stroking of the chin is an example of this.

● Distracting – when someone is constantly moving between different postures making it difficult to read the posture and the emotion.

● Placating – when hand signals are indicating acceptance of an emotion. This might be a hand pointing down to show acceptance or hands and arms open wide showing a welcoming approach.

● Levelling – when someone is trying to give the impression of being true and honest, using their hands a lot to communicate this. This can often be used also to be assertive and reassuring.

● Blaming – straightforward pointing and hand signals pointing in an assertive way. Body position may be half turned away from the person, showing distaste or disagreement.

Computing/Thinking

Placating

Levelling

Distracting

Blaming

Application

Emotional vocabulary

You will be beginning to see a reoccurring theme in this book about extending our vocabulary in order to effectively communicate how we feel. This is because without being able to locate, through language, the specific feelings we have, identifying the feeling and discussing it becomes almost impossible.

When talking to others about their feelings or trying to recognize a feeling, children need to draw upon as wide a vocabulary as possible. So while 'surprised' and 'shocked' may be similar, they are very much different and the feeling and response to each is very different. If children are unable to label and identify their legitimate feeling, they will often act out that feeling on others as a means for getting their needs met. However, while this is common in very young children, it is inappropriate behaviour as children get older. As such, children need to be able to communicate their feelings to be able to access strategic and focused help to get that need met as part of developing their social competence.

Developing an emotional vocabulary also allows children to recognize and read social clues that they see in others. An inability to read such social cues can ultimately result in a negative outcome, such as becoming an innocent victim of crime.

In addition, the ability to be discerning with the various emotional states such as sadness, anger or frustration requires an extended vocabulary of feeling words. For example, children may be either 'happy' or 'crazy' and miss all the subtle variations of feelings in between the two states.

Ultimately, a larger and more complex 'feelings vocabulary' allows children to make finer discriminations between the different feelings they have or observe, and as such are able to communicate with others about these states.

Advice

Below are 190 words (one word to discuss for every school day) that can be used to develop your own emotional and feelings vocabulary and that of your students.

acquiescent	afraid	affectionate	agitated	aggressive
amused	alarmed	angry	amazed	annoyed
animosity	anxious	apathetic	apprehensive	ardent
ashamed	awestruck	awful	awkward	bashful
bewildered	bitter	blissful	bored	brave
calm	caring	cautious	cheerful	comfortable
competent	competitive	concerned	confident	contemptuous
contented	cool	cordial	cowardly	critical
cross	curious	cynical	defeated	defensive
dejected	delighted	depressed	devoted	disappointed
discontented	discouraged	disgusted	disheartened	dismayed
dispassionate	disrespectful	distressed	distrustful	disturbed
docile	down	eager	edgy	earnest
elated	embarrassed	enjoyment	enthusiastic	envious
exasperated	excited	exhausted	expectant	fair
faithful	fatigued	fascinated	fearful	fidgety
forceful	forgiving	fractious	frantic	friendly
frightened	frivolous	frustrated	funny	furious
gentle	gloomy	grateful	greedy	grouchy
guilty	happy	hatred	hopeful	hopeless
hostile	humble	humorous	hysterical	impassive
impatient	impulsive	indifferent	inspired	interested
intolerant	irritated	jealous	joyful	kind
lazy	light-hearted	loving	meek	melancholic
nervous	obedient	optimistic	passionate	passive
pathetic	patient	peaceful	pessimistic	philosophical
pitiful	pleasant	pleased	poetical	pompous
proud	provocative	rapturous	reckless	regretful
relieved	reluctant	remorseful	repulsed	resentful
resilient	respectful	responsive	restful	restrained
revolted	ridiculous	righteous	romantic	sad
satisfied	sensitive	serene	shamed	shocked
shy	sincere	smug	spiteful	stimulated
stoical	stressful	stubborn	sulky	surprised
suspicious	sympathetic	tense	tolerant	tranquil
triumphant	trusting	uncaring	uncertain	understanding
unfair	unkind	unpleasant	unworried	upset
vain	vehement	worried	yucky	zany

The manipulating of emotions

As we are generally steered by our emotions, the ways our emotions are externally manipulated are open to question and examination. For instance, if you asked most people today what the biggest threat to them was then terrorism would possibly be high on their list. This is not an attempt to diminish what are genuine causes for concern. However, you are significantly more likely to do damage to yourself in your own home or while being treated in a hospital than suffer a terrorist attack. In essence, terrorism thrives on fear and plays on our emotions. In 1999 national statistics in the UK indicated that there were 200,000 injuries and 70 deaths from DIY.

Fear of strangers is another fear most of us have. It is an emotionally driven anxiety, yet you are statistically more likely to be killed by a member of your family than a stranger.

Road traffic accidents also remain a principal cause of accidental death and injury. Across the whole population in the United Kingdom in 1997 3,559 people were killed, 42,967 were seriously injured and 280,978 were slightly injured in road traffic accidents. Every year 1,500 car drivers and adult passengers die in road accidents and one hundred times that number are injured. And every year 1,000 or so adult pedestrians and cyclists are killed and 40,000 are injured. Each year in England nearly 180 children die and almost 4,800 are injured as pedestrians or cyclists. Many are killed when playing or walking close to their own homes. Added to this are the 215 deaths and 2,690 or more serious injuries to children riding as car passengers. Over 3,000 people aged over 65 years are killed annually in falls.

So many of our fears, some of which are innate, are often disproportionate to the probability. A war on terror may be convenient from a government and media perspective, fuelled and driven by our emotions, while a war on stepladders, driving, smoking and DIY may not have the same resonance.

Advice

Emotional news

Discuss the following with your students (obviously it may need adapting to a particular age).

The death toll from the London bombings in 2005 represents just six days of death on Britain's roads. The death toll from the Madrid bombings in 2004 represents merely 12 or 13 days of death on the Spanish roads. It is estimated that in 2007 more than 1.2 million people were killed in road accidents globally, the equivalent to more than one 9/11 taking place every day. Yet the public fear of terrorism – and the emotionally driven reaction to it – is on a completely different scale to that of death on the road.

From this we can see that the ways stories are given emphasis in the media are done so to create a maximum emotional impact. This is not to diminish the significance of the events; however, it is important that we are not misled by our emotions.

As a group activity, collect a series of newspapers on a particular day. Critique how the media manipulates the emotions and how they each approach stories in a different emotional way.

Application

43

Metaphors and stories

> 'Stories help us understand our lives – to explain who we are, what has happened to us and what might happen.'
>
> Corbett (2001)

Why do stories work so effectively at engaging us and stirring our emotions? Many teachers have often developed emotional literacy teaching skills, without recognizing it, through the telling of stories and use of metaphors. The use of narratives create a parallel life and helps us shape our emotional responses through helping us deal with situations that we hope we might or might not encounter.

Everyone loves a good story but it is felt that children particularly benefit from stories as they are considered to live closer to the world of subconscious feeling. This is why strong narratives and metaphors can touch children and get them to think in a way that complex arguments cannot. For instance, consider the difficult topics that are dealt with in the *Harry Potter* series. Fears and loss of parents, negotiation of meaning, development of friendships, anxiety and upheaval, yet delivered through a strong narrative they provide an engaging way to deal with complex and sophisticated topics.

Many schools now increasingly use storytellers (www.sfs.org.uk) as a means of passing on tales and values in a neutral and natural way to fill a gap in children's emotional learning. Such storytelling is rich in emotional impact and is a means to getting children to engage in complex topics that might otherwise be too difficult.

In addition to stories, metaphors can be equally powerful and effective as they help shape our understanding by linking abstract concepts to concrete language by:

- engaging the emotions;
- aiding memory of difficult concepts for all students (particularly special needs) by creating associations or links;
- helping learners to make sense of information and issues;
- developing an understanding about the way we as learners see things;
- allowing students to explore their feelings in a safe and non-judgemental way.

Advice

Emotions and metaphors in the classroom

Definition of a metaphor:

1 *A figure of speech in which a word or phrase that ordinarily designates one thing is used to designate another.*

2 *One thing conceived as representing another.*

You can use metaphors to:

● stimulate creative writing

● tell stories to discover meaning

● convey emotional information to the reader

● initiate deeper meaning

● engage learners in understanding their own emotions.

Think about how you can use metaphors (or other forms of expressive writing) to explore emotions by creating metaphors for some of the emotional words below. Discuss with the learners how the metaphors can sometimes work better at communicating a feeling and how they can be used as part of a narrative in storytelling.

For example: Anger = blowing a fuse, fuming, blowing his top, raising the roof, hitting the ceiling.

Emotion	Metaphors			
Sadness	For example, 'down in the dumps'			
	1	2	3	4
Love	For example, 'starry-eyed'			
	1	2	3	4
Happiness	For example, 'jumping for joy'			
	1	2	3	4
Fear	For example, 'shaking in her shoes'			
	1	2	3	4

Application

Emotional language: how are you feeling?

'Language exerts hidden power, like a moon on the tides.'

Rita Mae Brown

Emotional literacy involves developing awareness about our sense of self and worth, our internal feelings and our feelings towards others that we may or may not know. A key part of this is the language we use to convey our feelings and often a feeling can naturally be framed negatively as our emotional vocabulary is not sufficiently broad.

We don't however, as yet, fully understand how language shapes our emotions but what we do know is that language is a powerful force in learning and helping us deal with our emotions. Part of this lies in the brain appearing to have some difficulty dealing with complexity, and, as such, language in the form of metaphors and stories can help us. We also know that effective teachers use clever narratives and positive emotional language to engage learners and make them feel good. In fact a whole industry, based upon Neuro-Linguistic Programming, is fundamentally based upon language and influence.

What we do know is that having a good emotional vocabulary can make us feel better, as we are more accurately able to understand and locate our emotions. Also, the ability to view our emotions positively by turning negative emotional language into positive emotional language can have a profound effect on the way we feel. Children with a wider vocabulary also tend to be happier as they are able to feel more comfortable about themselves as they are able to communicate their feelings more effectively.

For example, although we might feel 'confused' by something, a more positive emotional framing of this would be 'curious', and while also we might feel 'scared' of a new task, a positive emotional perception of this is feeling 'challenged'. When learning, instead of 'I didn't do well enough', a positive framing would be 'I did the best I could and know I can do better'.

Positive emotions

This activity can be used in a variety of ways. First, you can simply use it to think about how you frame learning tasks and how you use positive emotive language to engage and challenge learners.

Second, the activity can be used with learners to get them to consider their emotional vocabulary; by first of all developing it and, second, learning how to re-frame feelings words from negative to positive.

Complete the table below by yourself or with your group, looking at how you can transform words by just thinking about them in a different way.

Negative emotion word	Alternative positive emotion word
insulted	misunderstood
disliked	underappreciated
unhappy	
frightened	
uncomfortable	
exhausted	
frustrated	
envious	
dejected	
indifferent	
fearful	
disappointed	

Emotion coaching: engaging or dismissive

'Feelings are much like waves, we can't stop them from coming but we can choose which one to surf.'

Martensson

It is important to acknowledge the significant way that our emotions are both mediated by and embedded in our language and those aspects of our language, as evidenced through activities such as Neuro-Linguistic Programming, work on our emotions in very subtle ways. It is also worth considering the attachment and additional value that is given to everyday emotive language, such as 'speaking from the heart', 'my gut feeling is' or 'I felt touched by'. What we feel, however, often guided by language, may not always be the best guide for our cognitive development or be in our best interests. Therefore, we all need to know a little bit more about how we are influenced.

Engaging or dismissing?

Research has shown that there can be two distinct types of emotional coaching which can be from friends, parents and teachers: emotion engaging and emotion dismissive.

Emotion dismissive is the type that views emotions negatively and merely as a distracter. This doesn't mean the emotion dismissive coach doesn't see, feel or acknowledge the emotion – it just means they will try to bypass or detract the emotion. Instead of focusing on the symptoms they will only focus on the short-term, well-intentioned, quick-fix solution. The problem with such an approach is that children tend to adopt the same approach, the way they were coached, so they will not give sufficient attention to their emotions and feelings, therefore developing a limited emotional palette.

Emotionally engaging coaching works slightly differently by discussing and exploring the emotion to try to understand the root cause of the feeling/emotion, rather than attempting to mask the emotion. This ultimately develops a stronger emotional vocabulary of understanding and a greater sense of empathy with others.

Advice

Engage or dismiss

Five steps for effective emotion coaching have been identified (Gottman) that we can all follow:

1   Notice emotions. Hone your ability, and that of your students, to read faces and voices and pick up on the specific ways in which emotion is expressed – even lower intensity ones.

2   View emotions in a positive light. See them as opportunities for teaching and intimacy.

3   Work to understand children's emotions. Offer validation and explain how you'd feel if you were in their shoes.

4   Provide verbal labels for emotions. Words and emotions are processed on different sides of the brain. Getting both sides to work together empowers a child to work through the feelings.

5   Set limits. Emotion coaching isn't a 'lovey-dovey' 'free-for-all' for kids. While all emotions are acceptable, not all behaviour is. Do not tolerate misbehaviour and share how bad behaviour makes you feel.

Application

Listening

A teacher was giving a lesson about the rainforest and said to the class that we are losing Brazilian rainforests every day. One little girl seemed to be quite emotional about the topic and on the way out asked her teacher, 'Exactly how many is a brazillion? It seems a lot.'

An important part of emotional literacy is the role of listening. While the previous sections have concentrated on communicating feelings, without the receiver actively listening, the extent of the communication is limited. Active listening is the ability to empathize and reflect when listening.

Have you ever attended a meeting and in the post-meeting discussion found that you took something completely different from the meeting than someone else? This kind of selective hearing is common, as when listening to others our brain is having to deal with a complex operation, often interpreting and decoding language that can be interpreted in many different ways.

For instance, 'I felt grumpy' could mean you were a little unhappy or you had just felt one of the seven dwarfs!

The first scenario is likely if you had been feeling a bit low recently, while the second could be true if you had just been to a pantomime. The reality is both could be true of the other situation, so you could also have been to a rubbish pantomime and lost your purse, so you were feeling a little grumpy.

Equally, it is not just what we say but how we say it that is also important. If saying 'I felt grumpy' with laughter in my voice and with a wicked grin on my face, we could probably guess I was talking about the pantomime scenario.

What this all means is that the listener, particularly when dealing with emotional scenarios, has to try and withhold a reactive response and must engage in reflective listening to try to get a fuller picture.

Speaking and listening

1 Envoys are a good way of developing effective and active listening in learners.

2 Split a class into groups of four to discuss a particular aspect of emotional literacy. For instance, it might be each group is discussing positive well-being.

3 The group discusses key aspects of the topic and comes up with their outcomes. For example, definition of well-being, what it means to be positive, someone they know who is positive, golden rules to staying positive.

4 Each person in each group takes a turn to visit another group for a set where someone from that group will discuss their outcomes. Notes are not allowed to be taken, except when they return back to their original place, where they must report back to their own group from the group they visited.

5 Each group presents back a synthesis of their findings after visiting the other groups.

The purpose of the exercise is to promote active listening, while also developing high level evaluative and synthesis thinking skills.

Application

Motivation: hooks and WIIFM

WIIFM = what's in it for me?

Our emotions and motivation are intricately intertwined as our emotions provide our ordinance system that drives us and motivates us based upon our emotional state. However, our motivations can also cloud our thinking and emotions. For instance, imagine you lost a very precious item – one that you were emotionally attached to. You would be highly motivated to keep searching over and over again in the same place where you thought you lost it. However, if you took an emotionally detached view you may be inclined to think from a wider perspective and look elsewhere. The classic example is if you play golf. It's always your partner who finds your lost ball as you are often too busy looking where you hoped it had gone.

In experiments extrinsic motivations have been found to distort our thinking and emotions. For example, in an experiment participants were asked to imagine a candle, some nails and a cigarette lighter and were asked how they would attach the candle to the wall using these three items. Those participants who were being rewarded for solving the problem took almost four minutes longer to come up with a solution than those given no reward. Those receiving no additional reward worked out fairly quickly to ignore the nails and to melt the candle and stick on the wall. It appears that extrinsic motivation can make us feel as if we need to try harder or overcomplicate when often a simple answer will do.

Therefore, within the learning context, it is important to stress the intrinsic reasons and motivations (what's in it for me) rather than the extrinsic (what you get because of this) motivations.

Advice

Mark Twain said it is easy to stop smoking – he had done it hundreds of times! The reality is that unless we are sufficiently emotionally engaged to do something it is unlikely we are going to change our behaviour or thinking.

Identifying hooks and WIIFM

Successful songs have a hook line or a hook tune – the bit that after hearing it on the radio you keep singing each day.

The same needs to be considered for successful emotional literacy in that teachers need to consider the hook line (the bit that children will remember) and the WIIFM line (the bit that motivates them to want to learn it, usually because of an emotional association). In the timetable below think about the week ahead and what the hook (H) and the WIIFM (W) for each lesson that you will be leading will be. (You might want to combine this with Teachers thinking about emotion, page 26.)

Another possibility is to get students to create their own one line emotional hook at the end of a lesson for reminding them what they have learned.

	Lesson 1	Lesson 2	Lesson 3	Lesson 4	Lesson 5
Monday	H: W:	H: W:	H: W:	H: W:	H: W:
Tuesday	H: W:	H: W:	H: W:	H: W:	H: W:
Wednesday	H: W:	H: W:	H: W:	H: W:	H: W:
Thursday	H: W:	H: W:	H: W:	H: W:	H: W:
Friday	H: W:	H: W:	H: W:	H: W:	H: W:

Application

Emotion and transition

Bungee jumping or bridge building?

How do you view the transition from primary to secondary school for pupils? Some schools take a bungee-jumping approach of 'close your eyes, away you go and I hope you survive'. Others take a more considered bridge-building approach where a pupil's transition is carefully navigated across the primary to secondary divide in a strategically planned manner.

The transition from primary to secondary school is one that is recognized as causing significant upheaval for children. The focus in recent years has primarily focused upon the transfer of cognitive and academic performance information rather than considering the emotional upheaval that many pupils face. Such a focus often fails to recognize the significant coping strategies required as children's anxiety may be heightened and self-esteem eroded as they move between two very different emotional environments.

The period of transition therefore has to be regarded as a significantly emotional one, which becomes heightened as many parents and teachers represent transition as a signal for arbitrary social change (from child to young person). For example, many parents will take their children to their primary school right up to the last day, accompanied by all the emotional support of talking, waving goodbye and hugging. In the secondary school, it is an expectation that students will make their own way, they will stand on their own two feet and their feelings will merely be regarded as transitional. For many children the emotional turmoil is greater than any academic one, but one which is merely disguised by the transition and a change of organizational and academic expectations.

Transition PowerPoint

When children move school there remains a focus on only transferring mostly academic information. Although this in itself is a positive part of the transition from one school to another, it must also be recognized that transition represents a significant emotional upheaval such as leaving friends, teachers, favourite views, sounds, smells and so on.

Many schools are now adopting new ways of dealing with transition including delivering the Year 7 curriculum in a similar manner to the Year 6 curriculum. This includes limiting the number of teachers that children are exposed to while students get used to their new surroundings. In such situations it is therefore important that the new teacher displays empathy with the new students and celebrates the transitions, while valuing and supporting children's feeling for these changes. Such activities might include:

- Considering Year 7 experiences to being more like the primary schools rather than trying to get the primary school like the secondary school.

- Instead of focusing purely on academic development when dealing with transition, consider the emotional developments necessary. What are the changes in expectations in terms of emotions and how are these communicated and developed?

- Although there may be a regular flow of academic information between the primary and secondary school, ask students to bring with them a 'Feelings PowerPoint', which they can share with their new teacher and new class. This might include favourite things about my primary school, my teachers and friends, and so on.

- Regularly dealing with 'what if?' scenarios. Many children will have heard many stories before they have entered the secondary school that may be causing them anxiety. It is important that regular 'what if?' scenario opportunities are run through so that they know what to do if something does go wrong.

Application

Getting the right emotional climate in the classroom

Two boys were arguing when the teacher entered the room. The teacher says, 'Why are you arguing?'

One boy answers, 'We found a £10 note and decided to give it to whoever could tell the biggest lie.'

'You should be ashamed of yourselves,' said the teacher. 'When I was your age I didn't even know what a lie was.'

The boys gave the £10 note to the teacher.

As a teacher have you ever had such a good classroom environment and a good relationship with the students that one of them feels such a sense of trust that they mistakenly call you 'Mum' or 'Dad', usually followed by howls of laughter from their friends and slight blushing? This is no accident as good teachers create a strong sense of trust and an emotional bond between themselves and their students, and this sense of trust actually creates an emotional chemical in the brain known as oxytocin. The stronger the indicator of trust, the more the oxytocin increases. When this is observed by others, trust can increase throughout members of a group, so your group will either all be with you or all against you.

The neurobiological mechanism that permits human beings to trust each other is not fully understood but, within the context of a school, trust is easily viewed between a variety of people: teacher and learner, teacher and teacher, teacher and parent, and so on. What has been found is that when someone observes that another person trusts them, oxytocin circulates in the brain and the body, and the stronger the indicator of trust, the more the oxytocin increases. What's more, if from this sense of trust comes a sense of success the brain creates dopamine as part of its reward system, making you feel good.

Creating trust

Trust is an essential element in any relationship, so it is important to think about how you create trust in your classroom.

One of the most important factors in creating trust is behaving consistently. This includes adopting clear routines and rituals for the class that may include how students enter and exit the room, how they interact with you and their peers, and what consistent sanctions are shared and applied. This does not mean an automaton response; it merely provides the cornerstones for the basis of your interactions with learners, while also providing motivation for students and developing their self-esteem.

The creation of trust and expectations is communicated through language and daily interactions developed over a period of time. This will include the consistent use of positive affirming language such as confirming your belief in a group through statements like:

- 'I know you are all capable of coming up with really good ideas.'
- 'There are some really good ideas coming out and you are all showing real signs of improvement.'
- 'The last lesson was fantastic and I don't expect anything less today.'
- 'There was some fantastic work today and I look forward to the next lesson to see how your ideas have developed.'

Application

Emotional communities of learning

'Coming together is a beginning. Keeping together is progress. Working together is success.'

Henry Ford

A community of learning is a group of learners who come together and learn from each other by sharing knowledge and experiences about the activities in which they are engaged. As such, learning to work collaboratively in such a community has to be an essential prerequisite of any education system. The success of the way we work together is, however, largely dependent on a whole range of factors, particularly communication, trust and engagement. Time must therefore be invested in developing positive emotional relationships if the success of a group is to be achieved.

Students must be encouraged to build a learning community where they feel responsible for including their peers and where they can develop the skills associated with building positive relationships, such as learning about making, breaking and sustaining friendships without hurting the feelings of others. When developing communities of learning, students also need to learn the skills of assertiveness so they become able to resist negative peer pressure, as well as developing a range of strategies to help them resolve conflicts before relationships are damaged or ill feeling escalates. Some key features in developing the correct emotional community include:

- Encouraging learners to use the words 'we' and 'our' to encourage inclusion and not exclusion.
- Encouraging learners to make sure that there is fairness – giving each their turn to contribute.
- Setting clear boundaries for behaviour such as: 'You are not allowed to hurt another student's feelings and other students are not allowed to hurt you.'
- Ensuring all learners are developing a wide emotional vocabulary to effectively communicate their feelings.
- Encouraging learners to try to read the emotions of others from their body positions and facial expressions and to act accordingly.
- Encouraging learners to give positive feedback when appropriate.

Advice

Fighting the ANTs

The degree to which an emotion is present within a community of learners depends on what feelings have been recently triggered. For example, if a student has had a terrible weekend or a negative experience with a previous teacher, he or she is more likely to be emotionally volatile and this is likely to spread within a group.

Therefore, there is a need for 'positive priming' to fight against ANTs (Automatic Negative Thoughts). ANTs are those negative thoughts that make us feel negative against someone or something, and often that negativity spreads and spirals out of control.

As teachers we can use four key tools for fighting ANTs:

1 sharing similar experiences
2 creating an emotional bond
3 creating a shared language
4 encouraging a sense of empathy.

With ANTs we need to re-frame any negativity in the following ways:

1 **Sharing similar experiences:** Explain how negative thought can be turned positive, for example 'Can anyone give me an example of when they have used a negative experience to motivate themselves?'

2 **Creating an emotional bond:** Explain how it is natural how we might be feeling and that often we may all be feeling the same way. Negative thoughts don't help us, so we need to work to support each other's feelings to make each of us feel better.

3 **Creating a shared language:** Often when fighting ANTs we lack the language to be able to identify the emotion/feeling. By using the exercises in this book an emotional vocabulary can be developed that enables a better understanding of each other's feelings and emotions to be developed.

4 **Encouraging empathy:** Understanding our own feelings and dealing with our own ANTs is one facet of emotional literacy. However, you can learn to understand other people's emotions through developing a sense of empathy. By working in areas 1, 2 and 3, emotional empathy should develop.

Application

Philosophy for children

Our emotions have traditionally been thought to be at war against reason and as such they have been thought to play a crucial role in what are taken to be typically irrational phenomena, such as wishful thinking and self-deception. Philosophy offers a way to find intermediate answers to challenge such states and asks questions we cannot fully answer, while challenging misconceptions we may hold.

Often when dealing with situations where big and difficult questions require a significant emotional investment, or when dealing with uncertainty, we need to suspend some of our belief systems that may make us feel uncomfortable. However, recognizing that big questions lead to uncertainty and emotional vulnerability is an important aspect of emotional literacy; we have to recognize that our brain and the subsequent emotions are not inclined towards deep meaningful thinking and this is why the feeling generated can sometimes be unpleasant.

Equally, as with many issues, there is a degree of sensitivity required when choosing topics that allow philosophical enquiry without upsetting the community within which the questioning takes place. This has to be a professional judgement and philosophical enquiry about religion, race and sexual orientation in some communities would be inappropriate.

Philosophy with children doesn't however have to be about Wittgenstein or Socrates, although naming the branch of philosophy will not be harmful; the focus should be on questions that we have some difficulty answering definitively.

Children do, however, make good philosophers because they have a strong sense of awe and wonder as they are creative, while being good at making connections. By developing philosophy in children the following occurs:

- Self-awareness – knowing what you are feeling and how it influences your thinking.
- Self-regulation – handling your emotions so they help rather than hinder your progress.
- Motivation – identifies what motivates you, while encouraging perseverance and the overcoming of setbacks.

Advice

Philosophical questions

There are no 'right' or 'wrong' answers with philosophical enquiry and the most important part is that learners are given the tools and emotional support to begin to frame questions, as well as starting to answer them. The important points are:

- that everyone has to be encouraged to contribute to the discussion
- that they develop good listening skills
- that they develop empathy for what others say
- that there is limited input from the facilitator.

My favourite entry point into philosophy is through Plato's allegory of the cave (just Google it if you are not familiar with it). The allegory gets us to question 'What is reality?' by using the cave as a metaphor for questioning our limited perceptions of reality. Therefore, the question is 'What is real?'

Some useful framing and extending questions might be:

- How do you know?
- Is it possible to know if that is true?
- Can you say more about that?
- What makes you say that?
- Do you have any evidence for that view?
- Does anyone else support that view?
- Is there another point of view?
- What would someone who disagreed with you say?
- How could you test to see if your thinking was true?
- Are we any closer to answering the question/problem?

Application

SEAL

Many teachers will have been introduced to the concept of emotional literacy by way of the Social and Emotional Aspects of Learning (SEAL) programme.

The underlying philosophy behind the SEAL programme is to develop an understanding of the relationship of learning with the social and emotional aspects of life. This is delivered through five key themes:

- self-awareness
- managing feelings
- motivation
- empathy
- social skills.

One of the most interesting parts of the SEAL programme is the early success reflected in improved behaviour as a result of a focus on the SEAL themes. Key to this is the recognition of the contribution to the development of the 'whole child'. This has led to reported benefits such as:

- better relationships within school between learners and teachers
- more consistent use of rewards and sanctions in the school behaviour system
- improved lesson planning considering the emotional aspects of learning
- a wider understanding of influences upon children's learning.

Central to these benefits are some key features, which include:

- increased respect for other's differences including strengths and weaknesses
- an increased focus on improved team working
- increased recognition and communication of feelings
- increased willingness to take risks in their learning.

Most importantly Ofsted, in their evaluation, reported that SEAL will be most effective where it is supported and understood by senior management teams and where it is 'embedded in the curriculum rather than bolted on to PSHE lessons'.

Advice

SEAL checklist

Use the checklist to consider some of the opportunities for implementing the SEAL programme.

Yes	No	
		SEAL materials are available for all teachers.
		Pupils and parents are fully aware of the decision to implement SEAL.
		Senior management understand and are involved in the implementation of SEAL.
		The criticisms of SEAL as well as the positive aspects of SEAL are understood.
		Staff understand how to deal with sensitive issues and pupils are informed of their right to withdraw from activities that are considered as sensitive.
		Opportunities are provided for older pupils to plan and deliver learning opportunities to their peers and younger pupils.
		SEAL is part of a disseminated and integrated approach rather than added to a single subject such as PSHE.
		Teachers are encouraged to plan for SEAL in all subjects and all subjects have a SEAL policy identifying SEAL opportunities and strategies.
		Sufficient time is given to all staff to develop understanding and expertise in SEAL including peer support and coaching.
		Links to developing SEAL extend beyond the school into the community.
		An ethos of well-being is extended to all members of the school community.
		Pupils play an active part in developing SEAL context, themes and policies.

Application

ECM

Every child really does matter!

One of the difficulties that many teachers face is initiative overload, and in addition to the SEAL programme we also have the big *Every Child Matters* (ECM) initiative also occupying schools. This might be enough to push any teacher over the edge. However, before you put the waste paper bin on your head and start making Dalek noises, there are similarities, which means these two initiatives are linked and can be delivered together.

SEAL, as we know, is linked to emotional development (as well as other social aspects) and emotional literacy, while the key themes of *Every Child Matters* are:

- being healthy
- staying safe
- enjoying and achieving
- making a positive contribution
- achieving economic well-being.

It is therefore clear that links between these two initiatives are natural and, if planned carefully, present a mutually supportive framework. In fact SEAL covers most of the ECM aims with the exception of specific topic-based activities from the PSHE and Citizenship Frameworks.

By completing the activity on the following page, you will be able to map out how the two initiatives can link within your school and within your subject using emotional literacy as the key focus. With both initiatives it is important to recognize that the best way for them to be developed is through contextualized and embedded approaches through subjects. This will make the activities meaningful rather than 'bolt on' and contrived activities.

Advice

Planning for SEAL and ECM

Consider how you can link SEAL and ECM with emotional literacy. This might seem complex but it should be a bit like a game of Sudoku. For each area of SEAL and ECM, list your three emotional literacy themes. You may even want to just put page references from this book. What you should see is that some aspects of emotional literacy are common or can be common to both ECM and SEAL. You will also see that some areas are not linked and might need covering elsewhere within the curriculum.

SEAL

Empathy	Social skills
1	1
2	2
3	3

Self-awareness	Managing feelings	Motivation
1	1	1
2	2	2
3	3	3

Be healthy	Stay safe	Enjoy and achieve
1	1	1
2	2	2
3	3	3

Make a positive contribution	Achieve economic well-being
1	1
2	2
3	3

ECM

Application

5

Self-awareness

Self-esteem, concept and efficacy

'Today you are You,
that is truer than true.
There is no one alive
who is Youer than You.'

Dr Seuss

Self-esteem is possibly the single most powerful force in our existence, as the way we feel and perceive ourselves affects virtually every aspect of our existence. Self-esteem is linked to our sense of worth and is best defined as 'a confidence and satisfaction in oneself' and is closely related to a person's self-concept, which relates to the 'mental image one has of oneself'. Self-esteem can therefore be considered to be evaluative of the value that a person places upon themselves. A further linkage that is closely related is the concept of self-efficacy, which refers to one's estimation of how well one can execute the necessary actions to deal with life events and activities, including learning. The relationship between these three areas is critical, as although you may have a good self-efficacy, it does not follow that a high self-esteem or self-concept will always follow. Such an imbalance can result in an impoverished view of the self, leading to emotional disengagement.

Ultimately, many of the activities in this book are aiming to get an ideal as well as realistic balance between positive self-efficacy, positive self-esteem and positive self-concept.

Advice

Central to emotional literacy is understanding how our emotions influence our self-perception and considering how we are largely responsible for selectively filtering what we choose to (or not to) see, hear and feel.

Using the BASIS model

First, there are no easy solutions when it comes to developing a positive self-image and it is likely that a variety of activities and experiences will need to be developed over a period of time. However, an important message early on within this context is that we are largely responsible for how we feel. As Eleanor Roosevelt said, 'No-one can make you feel inferior without your consent'. Therefore, what we choose to listen to and internalize will determine our self-concept, which will ultimately be reflected in our self-esteem and self-efficacy – positive or negative (if only it were so simple!). (See Appendix 2)

Second, the unfounded praising of someone purely focusing on the positive is unlikely to be the complete answer. Quick fix solutions may only produce short-term, sustainable gains. Therefore, long-term planning is an essential part of any self-esteem development.

BASIS:

- **B**elonging
- **A**spirations
- **S**afety
- **I**dentity
- **S**uccess

Who am I?

'I don't wish to be everything to everyone, but I would like to be something to someone.'

Javan

The Elton report in 1989 identified that many children in school whose behaviour and performance was considered poor were those whose self-esteem was threatened by their perceived failure within the school. Such children's own self-image became caricatures of the perceptions of others and, rather than participating in activities, it became easier for them simply not to take part. Challenging such self-fulfilling prophecies were central to the Elton report and were key to the call of making situations 'winnable' for such children. To break such self-fulfilling cycles of failure requires learners to re-conceive the various identities that they have in order to re-frame how they can make situations winnable. To correct such poor self-identity in learners requires identifying both their strengths and limitations. In doing so the often negative lens that children can view situations through can be challenged. So comments such as 'everybody hates me' and 'I'm rubbish at everything' can be slowly challenged and viewed through a more positive lens.

Artificial success within this context will, however, only be short lived so it is important that praise is grounded in achievement and that students reflect upon accurate information and are given realistic and achievable targets to build upon. In doing so learners need to reflect upon their feelings (extending their emotional vocabulary) and how this relates to their achievements, as ultimately it is how they feel and how they recognize these emotions that will drive their improvement.

Advice

Who am I?

These activities are about learners reflecting upon both emotions and how others may view them.

1   Create an emotional recipe for creating someone like you. Use the words on page 41 to create an emotional copy of yourself. Don't forget to include the quantities.

2   Pick a member of your family or friend and list five good things that they may say about you and three things about you that might annoy them.

3   Representing your feeling visually helps you understand the balance of your emotions. Create an emotional pie chart that shows your average emotions for a week (you could link this to your diary of feelings). Then create a pie chart based upon how your ideal emotions for the following week might look.

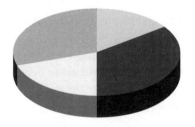

Friends and friendships

'Be who you are and say what you feel
because those who mind don't matter
and those who matter don't mind.'

Dr Seuss

It goes without saying that most of us were never taught how to make friends. It also goes without saying that most of us have friends who could have done with some lessons in friendship. Emotional literacy is therefore not just about ourselves but also about those that we interact with and, as such, the power of friendships and the emotional anxiety that comes from strains in friendships means that it is worth spending some time with children discussing how to shape their interactions with others and how to be a good friend. In doing so children are able to develop an understanding of themselves, as well as learning how to communicate clearly and to be assertive with the emerging confidence, enabling them to be positive agents of change.

Some possible topics and messages that can be explored with children include:

- Mediation is an important part of friendship – including discussing, negotiating and recognizing the ideal scenario is a win/win situation.

- Creating a realistic vision of friendship – including discussing what is realistic to expect from a friend and when being a friend.

- Belonging to groups – including maintaining a role within a group and how to deal with group involvement and separation.

- Repairing damaged relationships – including developing strategies such as prevention is better than cure.

- Being assertive when appropriate – including knowing what you value and recognizing the difference between being assertive and being aggressive.

- Achieving an appropriate level of independence – including recognizing when it is sometimes not right to let friendships control you and hold you back.

Advice

WACCA

When getting students to explore their friendships (particularly older students) and how they resolve conflicts, a useful model to guide discussion is the WACCA model. This is used in conflict resolution by identifying the boundaries of the relationships. The key principles of WACCA include:

- Weighting – to what extent is this person really a friend or just an acquaintance, as the answer may determine the extent of the investment in the remaining areas.

- Accommodation – the extent to which a person can and is willing to accommodate differences.

- Collaboration – the extent to which the two parties are willing and able to collaborate, including the willingness to collaborate in seeking a solution.

- Compromise – the extent to which both parties are willing to compromise.

- Avoidance – the extent to which both parties wish to avoid conflict and avoid further conflict.

With younger pupils a simpler method of getting them to frame their understanding of friendship is to get them to complete a simple friendship lens. For example:

- A friend is important to me because . . .
- A good friend makes you feel . . .
- A friendly person would always . . .
- A friendly thing that happened to me this week was . . .
- I was friendly this week because . . .
- I like to make my friends feel . . .
- My oldest friend is . . .
- My newest friend is . . .
- The quality I look for in friends is . . .

Application

Dealing with setbacks

*It's not how far you fall, **it's how high you bounce** when you reach bottom.*

If Michael Jordan, the basketball player, ever focused simply on the number of times he had missed the basket, then he would never have become one of the greatest basketball players in history. If James Dyson had focused purely on the number of setbacks he had when developing his revolutionary vacuum cleaner, he would never have become one of the world's most well-known designers. If J.K. Rowling only focused on the rejection letters she received, then we would never have had the *Harry Potter* series.

Although no one likes negative feedback or setbacks it is how we respond to such setbacks that is the most important. The difficulty with feedback is that we take it personally and then will often respond personally. For instance, in research as part of assessment for learning it was found that children who got a low mark would often not read the feedback as they felt it was merely further criticism adding more anguish to the process – even though the feedback was telling them how to get better.

In order for all children to attempt to view feedback, even though it is personal, as a positive way to improvement means removing personalities from the situation. So, although some children will often feel it is all teachers picking upon them and all of the time, the reality is often different. Therefore, a process of re-framing is necessary to focus on what needs to change and why, rather than blanket statements of despondency. Negative or critical feedback must therefore be viewed as providing the key to unlocking the path to improvement, while no feedback or limited feedback keeps the path locked.

One final point to remember is that most of the time difficult feedback is given by someone because they care and because they are not willing to take the easy option of merely saying something palatable. Why? Because it often takes a lot longer and is a lot more difficult to give what is perceived by the receiver as negative feedback.

Advice

Re-framing feedback

'It is OK to fail, but it is not OK to give up.'

Kate (age 8)

There are three essential parts to emotional literacy that can be applied to most situations:

1   The ability to understand our own emotions and to empathize with others.
2   The ability to listen to others.
3   The ability to express our emotions effectively.

When dealing with setbacks we can use these parts to help frame some essential questions that the learner must ask to deal with the setback:

1   Do I have any actual evidence that someone does not like me and is deliberately giving me poor feedback?
2   How can I find out? Have I spoken and listened to the person?
3   Can I use their feedback to improve?
4   What three steps do I need to do next to improve?

By re-framing the often perceived negative feedback learners can begin to focus on what matters, rather than being sidetracked on focusing on personalities and indifferences.

Boys and emotional literacy

Give a boy enough rope and he will come back with a dog!

The topic of boys and emotional literacy is a large one as many feel that it is in fact boys' emotions that are the root cause of what is considered the underachievement of boys. Within this context it is important to remember several key points. First, the underachievement debate is a complex one and the labelling of boys as failures does little to help boys' self-esteem, which is often more vulnerable than it may appear.

Second, boys are products of their evolution and their environment. In many ways they are pre-programmed to behave in the way that they do and in a different context those very attributes that frustrate teachers are what are required to help us survive. The control boys have over their emotional life may, however, appear to be impaired, with their impulsive emotions often overriding and overwhelming their rational self. However, within a secure and nurturing environment boys are able to successfully develop their emotionally literacy.

Research tells us that boys' innate emotional abilities are different than girls – so we should not expect the same. Girls' brains develop quicker and earlier than boys, while the ability of boys to read emotions does not appear to be as developed as in girls.

Of course these are large generalizations but what is true is that boys are emotionally vulnerable as part of a changing male culture, as the role of the male in society is a constantly changing one which can increase the sense of vulnerability. This is manifest with high levels of suicide among young males, high crime rates and high drop-out rates from school as the traditional employment routes, family role and notions of masculinities are challenged.

Part of these difficulties lie in the juxtaposing of the realities with the desirables. While it is OK for boys to display anger, how this is communicated within a modern society is less clear. It is therefore important that we don't illegitimatize natural behaviour (as suppression can do more harm than good) but that we use emotional literacy to enable boys to better understand themselves.

Advice

Developing a policy and strategies

With any discussion on gender it is important to avoid generalizations and stereotypes, and therefore it is important to know the boys in your school environment. What we know is that not all boys are underachieving and lots of boys have a positive emotional well-being. However, we also know that many boys find it difficult to communicate their emotions and feelings outside of their peer groups, and it is therefore important that schools develop policies and strategies that suit their students, using evidence from their students to inform their practice.

Three themes that have been shown to work favourably with boys include:

- **Enhancing communication.** This includes developing boys' emotional vocabulary, as well as developing alternative ways of communicating when dealing with sensitive issues. Activities such as email mentoring have been shown to help, with some schools finding that using different forms of communication helps boys who may find it difficult communicating face to face.

- **Recognizing innate behaviour.** Many of the sometimes frustrating behaviours that boys display are innate and there is a need to go some way to recognizing this. Equally boys need to understand how some of their behaviour is considered incompatible within modern society and how they should be receptive to the feelings of others.

- **Challenging inappropriate conceptions of masculinity.** Many boys merely reproduce the behaviour of those around them, which they see from family and friends. Such behaviour when played out in the education environment, such as aggression and bullying, is inappropriate and it is important that boys become aware that there are alternative and more valued conceptions of masculinity.

Application

Pupil voice

Very much part of the *Every Child Matters* and the Personalized Learning agendas is the theme of pupil voice, which ties into the Ofsted programme of inspections that now takes into account learner's perceptions of their schooling.

For many, this goes against the grain of the way most adults were brought up, which was 'to be seen but not heard', and many teachers feel vulnerable at the thought of pupils giving the 'low down' on their teaching. For some teachers there may even be a feeling of resentment as asking pupils their opinion gives them the appearance of an elevated status, creating a 'them against us' scenario.

However, there is a significant misconception about a pupil's voice and that is just because a pupil says something, it doesn't mean they are right. What it does is provide a rich insight into a pupil's perceptions, as they are in effect expert witnesses. Ultimately, this can provide incredibly valuable information about a pupil's beliefs, misconceptions and feelings towards the school.

In essence, it provides a shortcut way to finding things out quickly – that which otherwise may go unknown – and an essential part of this is the development of a pupil's emotional vocabulary (so they can externalize their feelings) and emotional literacy (so that they can understand why they feel the way they do).

Pupil voice now fits neatly into national programmes including the guidance documents for personal, social and health education (PSHE), social and emotional aspects of learning (SEAL) and the national healthy schools standard (NHSS) which includes recognition of the value of participating in whole-class discussion, and which encourages the active participation of learners while recognizing the value of pupil voice. The benefits of such pupil engagement are significant and relate to emotional well-being, self-development and emotional engagement with the curriculum and culture of the school.

Advice

Pupil voice participation

A key feature of pupil voice is avoiding the often tenuous and contrived school councils, which merely serve a purpose of meeting a target rather than a genuine opportunity for engaging learners in discussions about their school.

For this to happen there has to be opportunities for:

- pupil autonomy – they have a clear role in setting the agenda
- pupil self-management – which inevitably means the opportunity for things to go wrong
- emotional engagement – there has to a feeling that taking part is worthwhile.

A range of possible activities rich in pupil voice participation include:

- buddying systems
- peer tutoring
- peer teaching
- circle time
- student governors
- students on appointment panels
- school improvement plans
- healthy schools
- classroom observation
- student as co-researchers
- student-led learning walks
- students-as-researchers
- students evaluating work units
- classroom consultation.

Motivation

'Motivation is a fire from within. If someone else tries to light that fire under you, chances are it will burn very briefly.'

Covey

Have you ever wanted something really badly such as a gadget, new clothes, car and so on, and everything you do seems to make you think of that something more and more? Every time you watch the television, read a newspaper or speak to someone, there appears to be a reminder of that object that you really wanted. This happens not because the world has dramatically changed but because you are sufficiently emotionally engaged and motivated to make connections that you would not normally make. You have become attuned to the breadth of connections, all making a more convincing argument for you to get your desired object.

This happens due to the strong links between emotion and motivation as it is our wonder, curiosity and urges to discover that drives our motivational instincts. Our emotions therefore direct our attention and give us the impetus to maintain energy in the pursuit and commitment to a task.

For teachers the challenge is to motivate children so that they become sufficiently self-motivated themselves, as we know that that intrinsic motivation is a much more powerful and sustainable force than any external motivation. For this teachers need to consider how to emotionally engage learners by either making personal links and connections or getting students to make their own connections to activities and topics. This might include using narratives and stories as well as hooks and WIIFM to motivate through emotional engagement.

MOTIVATE

We know that intrinsic motivation is more effective than extrinsic motivation. However, when dealing with a topic it is likely that the teacher will make the first connections for the learner. Use this model to both plan and focus attention on building emotional engagement.

M = make links for students to a topic that has a level of emotional engagement

O = observe how students respond and adjust if necessary

T = take time to think about further emotional connections with the topic

I = if it is not working, adjust

V = verify through question and answer student's emotional engagement, such as 'how do you feel about . . .?'

A = accept that not all students all of the time will be emotionally engaged

T = think about alternative methods for emotionally engaging such as visual stimulus, audio, role-play narratives, hooks and WIIFM

E = evaluate and adjust

Values: from narcissism to altruism

We can't help everyone, but everyone can help someone.

Have you ever not stopped to give help to someone in the street? Why is it we help people sometimes and not on other occasions? It has been determined that it is not whether we are 'good' or 'bad' people and not that we simply don't want to, it is just that we don't always see the need at that particularly time as we might normally see it. Our emotional focus is elsewhere. One of the key features of emotional literacy is adjusting this focus.

Neuroscience suggests that our default brain state is ultimately defaulted to a help state – we enjoy helping others. Therefore, we naturally empathize and our mirror neurons act almost like Wi-Fi matching those that we help, giving us that positive feeling. For many children, however, because of the values that may have been instilled in them, they don't feel obliged to help others and may reject the emotional engagement that comes with helping someone in favour of a purely selfish indulgence.

The reason we don't help others lies somewhere on a scale from complete self-absorption to complete empathy. Preoccupation with the self is natural and shouldn't be completely rejected. However, not displaying any empathy at all can result in broken relationships and a lack of engagement with friends and peers. Emotional literacy therefore allows us to discuss and consider our compassionate, ethical and virtuous decision making and challenges the self-rationalizing preoccupation trance that we all have at times.

Advice

Values

Group discussions are a useful way of exploring the extent to which we feel we should help others. Below is a difficult scenario (of which there are many versions), which can be used as a discussion and is used in experimental philosophy to examine how our values shape our decision making.

John is the only passenger in the front carriage of a train on some elevated tracks; the conductor is alive but has passed out over the controls. John knows about underground trains and knows that the automatic braking system at the next station will stop the train, so John, the conductor and the other passengers are not in danger. But he sees that the train is speeding toward five people working ahead on the tracks; the tracks are so high that they cannot escape in time. John also sees that if he can pull down the emergency brake lever located under the control panel, the train will stop before it hits the five workers. The train's cockpit is so narrow that the only way to get to the brake lever in time is to push the conductor off the controls and out of the doorway of the speeding train. The only way for John to prevent the deaths of the five workers on the main track is to push the conductor out of the train in order to pull down the brake lever. If John pushes the conductor out of the train, the conductor will be killed by the impact. If John does nothing, the five workers will be run over and killed. What should he do – how can he make a decision?

Walking the talk: sustainability

In this book I have tried to provide you with lots of ideas that will make your students increasingly emotionally literate. However, the only way you can sustain emotional literacy is through committing to a whole-school approach. This means that everyone in and around the school has both an understanding of and commitment to the concept of emotional literacy. This includes parents, teachers (including part time, supply and trainee), support staff, governors and management teams. With emotional literacy, however, it is not just what people say or what is written in policies, but how individuals conduct themselves in an emotionally literate environment. Ultimately, this means 'walking the talk'. There is little value in saying one thing and then behaving in a contradictory fashion. Central to this is the 'growing' of an emotional literacy policy, the term 'growing' being important as it is unlikely that any off-the-shelf policy will suffice. Therefore, the emotional literacy policy for your school has to be one that grows over the years and is adjusted when necessary. You may also want to start small, with a particular year group or with a particular group of committed teachers. Most importantly, there has to be time for reflection and development. Remember, emotional literacy is not a gimmick. What can be more important than your students' happiness and emotional well-being? Equally, what better foundation can there be from which to build learning than a firm foundation built upon students' well-being!

Advice

Developing a policy

The first five steps to developing an emotional literacy policy are:

1   Audit. Identify what is going on already related to emotional literacy.

2   Where are the gaps and what is the overall picture? Is it skewed in any way?

3   Develop a strategy that builds upon existing good practice and balances out any inadequacies.

4   Introduce additional practices where necessary.

5   Commit to sustainability through development, promotion and revisiting of a policy.

The five key principles of developing an emotional literacy policy are:

1   This is not a policy for some but for all members of your school community.

2   The best policies grow over time rather than simply being implemented.

3   Start small and work up.

4   Communication and reflection are critical.

5   Remember the big picture. This is about students' well-being, not just about developing a policy.

Application

Anchors away...

'If you realized how powerful your thoughts are, you would
never think a negative thought.'

Anon.

Have you ever felt quite negative about a colleague or student whom
you simply don't have a positive word for and who you just don't
seem to get on with? I once had a tutor at university who I didn't
really like and, as much as I knew that I was trying to get on with
him, the relationship steadily got worse. This was a classic example of
anchoring – where I had associated negative feelings to a person and
no matter what he said my first instinct was to think he was wrong,
while subconsciously I am sure my body language and interactions
were equally negative.

I decided I needed to change so I wrote in the top of my diary every
day an acronym that was a constant reminder that I had to be positive.
Remarkably it worked! I did start to feel positive and most importantly
developed a good working relationship with my tutor.

The power of anchoring should also not be underestimated. For
instance, the whole concept of celebrity endorsement relies heavily on
subconscious anchoring in that we associate positive feeling towards
the celebrity, which rubs off and anchors to the product.

Therefore, subconsciously we all tend to anchor certain emotions to
certain events – positive or negative. However, with anchoring, we can
often associate negativity to events that can be damaging to us. Even
worse, unlike my scenario where I knew exactly what was causing my
difficulties, many of us don't realize where the negativity is associated
and therefore take a global view such as it is all work, all students or
all family causing distress, when it is usually only one tiny facet of our
interactions.

Advice

Diary of anchors

This is an exercise for teachers and students.

It is important that when we adopt a negative anchor we try to identify what it is that causes our negativity and what can be done about it. It is therefore important that we try to be specific and to do this we need to reflect on who, what and why are the causes of the negative feelings. This can be done by both you and your students as a means to identifying and relocating your emotional anchors.

One effective way of doing this is to keep a diary of feelings, but instead of a traditional diary, divide the page in two so that one side is the usual descriptive events and the other is headed 'feelings'.

Try to attach precise feelings to precise events to identify what it is that make you feel in that way (you might want to use some of the words from 190, page 41).

After a period of time you should see a pattern emerge, with certain emotions associated with either a person or an event. It will only be through rationalizing these emotions and these events that you can begin to change your feelings (assuming you wish to). Set yourself a reminder of how you want to feel when these events occur and monitor the changes in your diary.

Deferring gratification

'You have brains in your head.
You have feet in your shoes.
You can steer yourself,
any direction you choose.'

Dr Seuss

Motivating oneself and managing our emotions while also pursuing our goals makes huge emotional demands upon an individual. Such emotional self-management and control is often against our first instincts and we have to overcome our impulsiveness by deferring our immediate gratification. This is an important part of emotional literacy and a valuable lesson for all children.

In research studies, the ability to defer gratification by decreasing impulsivity has been considered a form of intelligent behaviour. Monitoring one's own behaviour and developing strategies to be able to defer is a lifelong valuable capability.

Anchoring, re-framing and visioning are all useful methods when developing increased consciousness in order to defer immediate gratification. This means thinking about what we are feeling, from breathing to facial expressions to muscle tension, thinking about the consequences of impulsiveness and thinking of the benefits derived from deferring our impulsivity.

For instance, to some hunger and anxiety might feel the same, with both requiring a different response. Equally, often we will crave certain foods (due to some outdated wiring in our brains), particularly foods high in fat or sugar, when these are really not needed and which are potentially harmful.

Extending this further, certain professions such as firefighters and the police have to train to overcome their impulsive instincts, while also knowing at times that they have to rely on their instincts for survival. For instance, a firefighter entering a burning building makes little sense to a brain built for survival, while for the police distinguishing between a toy gun and a real gun might not make much sense to their instincts – in which case they need to overcome their impulsive nature through a process of rationalizing.

Advice

Marshmallow test

One of the most famous diagnostic studies of impulse control and delayed gratification is the marshmallow test. In the test, pre-school children were sat at a table on which was placed a marshmallow. An adult advised that if they did not eat the sweet until the adult returned after a few minutes, they would be given two further marshmallows – a test of their ability to resist their impulses.

In the follow-up study carried out when the children were aged up to 15 years old, the children that were able to wait as pre-schoolers were children that were described by their parents as being more socially competent, they had more friends, they were more outgoing and their academic performance was better as they tended to cope with problems better than children who were unable to wait their turn and who acted impulsively!

So try a deferred gratification experiment with your group, for example involving homework, break time, time off an activity and so on. Remember, there are no hard and fast rules to this. It is not guaranteed and it should not lead to labelling of students! However, it is worth sharing the findings and discussing the concept of deferring with your group, as well as discussing when and when not to act upon your impulses.

Cultures and subcultures

Parts of our feelings are innate. They just happen and are hard wired into our brains, while others can be considered as cultural in that they are shaped by our environment. Much of this cultural transmission reinforces what we do and what we think based upon reproducing certain behaviours linked to our emotions. In fact, a term has been created called 'memes', which is the cultural equivalent of gene replication. So everything you have learned by copying (consciously or subconsciously) from someone else is a meme; every word, every catchphrase, every story you have ever heard and every song you know is a meme and as such they are a powerful medium for cultural influence and shaping our feelings.

So why do you wear those trainers? To create a certain look, to be able to be identified as part of a particular culture? Even if not consciously, subconsciously our feelings are guiding us into certain types of feelings and behaviours.

The shaping of our conscious and subconscious behaviour has, however, undergone a radical shift in the last 20 years and the copying of behaviours, tunes and actions has been significantly enhanced through email and through websites such as YouTube, MySpace and Facebook. For example, the most viewed video on YouTube for 2006/07 was the 'evolution of dance', with over 80 million people watching it in just over a year. By mentioning it I have just propagated it!

With memes, however, it is not always the best ideas or the most productive behaviours that get propagated; it is the best fit at that time. Why else would people have ever worn Afghan coats or hot pants? Because they were a cultural fit at the right time!

Cultural reproduction is not, however, just about clothes. It is also about the group endorsement of certain potentially negative attitudes and behaviours, such as substance abuse, drug taking and fast driving, and as such they are not always conducive to a person's well-being.

Memes part of a crowd

Part of the concept of memes is recognizing that just because something has gathered a certain momentum, it doesn't mean it is right. (It equally doesn't mean it is wrong.)

The point is that only through children thinking and reflecting will they recognize how much they are being emotionally manipulated.

So while perhaps innocent fun, the latest fads are an illustration of how our emotions are manipulated. We want to be like everyone else and as such children can be exploited (commercially) or they may adopt behaviours not conducive to their well-being (such as under-age drinking, obesity, and so on).

It is worth discussing the evolution of fads and how they often make little sense. In particular it is worth talking about how fads from the past now seem ridiculous. Two current fads below can be used to start the discussion.

Why do some people wear their baseball cap backwards, high up or at strange angles?

First, caps are an affiliation to a team and a sport that can be considered tribal behaviours and is worthy of discussion. However, the wearing of a cap that is meant to shade the eyes in a way that is deliberately not shading the eyes is a means of communicating resistance. Although most children won't recognize this, it is a message that 'I am part of a group but that I can suffer the difficulties of not shading my eyes in preference to communicating I am a conventional supporter of a team'.

Why do some people wear their trousers hanging below their waist?

This again is another cultural phenomenon. Traditionally, we wear trousers to protect our modesty and most of us would be horrified at showing our underwear in public. However, the wearing of trousers below the waist, so they look as if they are falling off, comes from the prison culture where belts are removed when prisoners are in detention. This type of fashion has gathered a momentum and again many children adopting the fashion would not be aware of the messages that such a fashion presents.

Application

Getting ready for examinations

'Operator! Give me the number for 911!'

Homer Simpson

I have over the years foolishly dragged myself out onto a rugby pitch on a Saturday afternoon and watched perfectly reasonable adult male brains turn to jelly as their decision-making capabilities leaves them as they cross the white line. What's more I have watched perfectly intelligent, high achieving males lose all sense of reasoning and thinking when put under pressure. None more so than an ex-captain (whose nickname became Chaos) who, under pressure, completely lost the power to count and regularly we would start the second half with too few or too many players.

The point is that stress affects our thinking and as noted early on in this book, the hijacking by the amygdala redirects our attention from rational thinking when under stress.

In schools there are few more stressful occasions than examination time – the culmination of all the years of hard work being assessed in one very small window (crazy isn't it?). However well prepared your students are for their exams, many can simply be overwhelmed by the examinations. For some the anxiety will be too great and can severely affect their performance.

Within this context it is worth considering why we have anxiety and feel stress. It is simply our emotions informing us that this is not a particularly pleasant experience so the anxiety, uncertainty and nausea are all by-products of the chemicals in our brain trying to tell us 'don't go any further'. However, we can also use these feelings productively and students have to know that the feelings of stress and anxiety are also preparing them for something (although exam anxiety is not a specific form of evolutionary response).

These feelings will, however, be generally relatively short-lived and are a good sign that they are taking the exams seriously. These feelings are also the means to tapping into their potential to get the best out of themselves by channelling their energy into the short-term task of preparation for their exam.

Advice

Examination preparation

Some points to consider with your examination groups:

1 **Getting ready** Being nervous is a natural reaction. It is a sign that the brain is preparing for something and it is better to have some rather than no nervousness. Confidence and reassurance will come from being well prepared. However, because the stakes are high, it is natural that there will be some stress and tension. The key is to recognize this in positive terms and put the anxieties to positive use.

2 **Preparation** It is important that when students are nearing examination time, the process of examinations is demystified as much as possible. This includes taking students through the process of where they will be taking exams, what it will be like and what they can take in with them.

3 **Preparation** It is good to pair up learners with others in their group so that they have some 'revision buddies' that can help by talking about how their revision is developing. Get ex-students to come along, who have been in a similar position, to calmly reassure the students, as well as alerting them to some of the realities.

4 **Preparation** It is also important to talk to students about fears as they arise and offer them opportunities to discuss their concerns anonymously. These can then be further addressed through the whole class so that all can benefit from the reassurance.

5 **Sleep and food** The brain needs good quality sleep in the run-up to exams. Cramming can have a negative effect and the more sleep learners get the better. Also eating the right food is important. The brain will naturally want high fat and high sugar but these will not optimize brain-function.

6 **Post exams** Think about using post-exam periods to learn from the experience. How did they feel and what coping strategies did they find useful? It is worth reflecting upon the anxieties as it can be virtually guaranteed that they will be revisiting those feelings throughout their lives.

Application

Emotional knowledge

Emotional intelligence

First, we had IQ, which education and business were firmly built upon using the method of intelligence testing as a basis of selecting those with notionally high intelligence. Then we had Howard Gardner suggesting that we have strengths in any number of the nine intelligences that he describes as multiple intelligences. From this grew EQ, Daniel Goleman's concept of emotional intelligence. Goleman suggests that you can be a genius but lack the social and emotional capacity to convey ideas and operate effectively in the education and work environments.

Some would say that emotional intelligence is an oxymoron, as our feelings and emotions are far from rational and intelligent.

Goleman's work is, however, very close to emotional literacy and the five themes for the basis of EQ are:

1   awareness of what you're feeling
2   managing your emotions
3   self-motivation
4   ability to empathize
5   assimilating these skills.

Ultimately, to interact more effectively with others, you need to become more emotionally intelligent. In doing so it pays to challenge the thoughts that trigger our feelings of uncertainty, fear, anger and so on. This means that our emotions are not just about what happens, it is also about how we think about it.

Advice

Emotional literacy is just one part of the growing interest that is occurring in relation to emotion in education. Other areas are briefly discussed in this chapter, in order that you can begin to develop a breadth of understanding relating to emotion.

Awareness of feelings

Emotional self-awareness is the ability to recognize one's feelings and act upon them. This simple activity helps students frame their self-awareness by completing the statements about how they feel in the spaces below.

This can then be used as the basis of teacher/student discussions or paired discussions.

Complete each statement based on how you feel. Complete the blank spaces and add your own feelings (you may want to use the words from the Emotional word list, page 41).

When I am happy I feel _____ and _____.

When I am sad I feel _____ and _____.

When I am embarrassed I feel _____ and _____.

The way I want to feel is _____ and _____.

My friends make me feel _____ and _____.

My family makes me feel _____ and _____.

My teachers make me feel _____ and _____.

Asking for help makes me feel _____ and _____.

Talking to others makes me feel _____ and _____.

Meeting new people makes me feel _____ and _____.

Trying new things makes me feel _____ and _____.

Application

Creativity and emotion

'Come to the edge, he said.
They said: We are afraid.
Come to the edge, he said.
They came. He pushed them and they flew.'

Guillaume Apollinaire

In almost all of the literature relating to creativity the concepts of risk and uncertainty are considered to be paramount in a creative experience. But how does the brain deal with uncertainty, anxiety and risk? Ultimately, the brain is built for survival and it will always resort to this default state when there is a sense of fear or anxiety. Unfortunately, with creativity the conditions that we operate under are very close to these areas. Often we are having to work in very uncertain and risky ways creating a chemical called acetylcholine in the brain, which creates that unpleasant feeling, 'butterflies in the tummy', of not knowing how to proceed. In such situations the amygdale, which is responsible for the 'fight or flight' syndrome within the brain, can override the thinking part of the brain, resulting in a lack of creative response as it struggles to regain a sense of certainty.

Therefore, within the learning and creative environment there has to be a strong sense of trust between the teacher and students, and this sense of trust actually creates a further chemical in the brain known as oxytocin. The stronger the indicator of trust, the more the oxytocin increases and when this is observed by others trust can increase throughout members of a group. Therefore, your group will either all be with you or all against you. What has also been found is that when someone observes that another person trusts them, oxytocin circulates the brain and the body.

The stronger the indicator of trust, the more the oxytocin increases. What's more, if from this sense of trust comes a sense of success, the brain creates dopamine as part of its reward system – making you feel good.

These chemical reactions can be considered as creative emotions and feelings and neurobiology is now shedding light on the phenomena that we previously didn't understand.

Advice

Three Ps

Next time you are trying to encourage a creative learning environment use the three Ps creative emotional model: **P**erson, **P**rocess and **P**roduct.

- **Person** Think about the learner's emotional needs in order for them to be creative. This includes using language that reduces some of the stress that comes from being creative. Therefore, you might use sayings such as:

  Don't worry about what you think is right . . .
  It's good to take risks . . .
  Feel free to explore your ideas . . .

  This stage also includes avoiding the emotional inhibitors of creativity such as criticism in the early ideas stage, time pressures and extrinsic motivation, for example 'You need to do X to get a grade C'.

- **Process** Within this stage is the emphasis on making the emotional connection between the student and the learning contexts. This means the teacher choosing contexts that the student can emotionally relate to and engage with; choosing or creating an emotional bridge to engaging contexts increases the learner's intrinsic motivation.

  Within this stage it is useful to ask questions such as:

  - How would you feel if?
  - How do you feel about X?
  - What do you think X feels?

- **Product** The product stage is concerned with the learner thinking about the person or persons who will receive the outcomes of their creative outcomes, whether this is through a drawing, story, music, design or dance. Within the product stage it is the purposeful consideration of the receiver's emotions that are at the heart of the learner's decision making. Therefore, questions might be:

  How do you want X to feel when they use/see/hear your outcome?
  To what extent do you want them to feel happy/sad/safe/and so on?
  How else might you make them feel X?

Application

Phobias

FEAR is an acronym in the English language for 'False Evidence Appearing Real'

Donald

There are estimated to be around ten million people who suffer from phobias in the UK, the most common being social phobias (such as fear of public speaking), which accounts for approximately two million people. Phobias are rooted in our reactive emotions. They are the automatic responses to situations or objects that overcome our rational thinking, forcing us to adapt our behaviour and often associated with negative outcomes such as not doing something because of the fear associated with the event. Some consider phobias to be evolutionary while others consider them to be the result of peculiarities or damage to specific emotional systems. For example, 'hippopotomonstrosesquippedaliophobia' is an abnormal and irrational fear of long words, while 'phobophobia' is a fear of phobias itself.

The evolutionary perspective of phobias is, however, interesting as it allows us to rationalize values and recognize phobias rather than merely rejecting them as irrational. So a fear of heights, enclosed spaces, spiders and snakes can all be rationalized as highly attuned survival response systems.

Most phobics will avoid their fears, which can have the effect of increasing the phobia by psychologically increasing the belief in the danger. Given such numbers of people with phobias then it is almost certain that there will be children within your class who have phobias that may not be recognized as such, but which are intense, irrational fears of certain things or situations (for example, dogs, bees, injections, the dark, flying and so on). Children may not realize that their fears of such objects are disproportionate and unreasonable and as such children with phobias should be referred for specialist help and support. The teacher's role is therefore one of raising awareness and identifying and recognizing children who may be suffering from phobias, as well as providing reassurances and awareness through discussing and contextualizing phobias and fear.

Advice

Contextualizing phobias and fears

By discussing fears and phobias, teachers can both help contextualize and rationalize children's fears. Contextualization can be delivered through discussing how fear and phobia is dealt with in classic literature and quotes. Use the examples below to discuss the way the various writers have rationalized and examined fear, while getting students to also examine their own fears.

'The only thing we have to fear is fear itself.'

Franklin D. Roosevelt

'I have almost forgot the taste of fears:
The time has been my senses would have cool'd
To hear a night-shriek, and my fell of hair
Would at a dismal treatise rouse and stir
As life were in't: I have supp'd full with horrors;
Direness, familiar to my slaught'rous thoughts,
Cannot once start me.'

Will, *Macbeth*

'I must not fear. Fear is the mind-killer. Fear is the little-death that brings total obliteration. I will face my fear. I will permit it to pass over me and through me. And when it has gone past I will turn the inner eye to see its path. Where the fear has gone there will be nothing. Only I will remain.'

Frank Herbert, *Dune*, 'Litany Against Fear', 1965

'What are fears but voices airy?
Whispering harm where harm is not.
And deluding the unwary
Till the fatal bolt is shot!'

Wordsworth

Application

Pedagogy of discomfort

A possible misconception about emotional literacy is that it is all about making life easy: 'rose tinted spectacles' and 'home baked apple pie'. However, we all know that life just isn't going to be easy and in some cases making someone's life easier can actually be detrimental to them.

For example, not long ago I was told about the design of a new building for severely disabled children who had a whole range of physical and visual sensory problems. Many could barely walk or see.

When the new school was being built the headteacher insisted the designers create the most uneven floor with significant undulations and changes in texture every 10 cm. I was quite surprised by this and felt that the opposite might be more appropriate – perhaps thick carpet to protect the children if they fell. This was until it was explained to me that if they took my approach it would be better for the children in the short term but in the long term it would only serve to institutionalize them. The most demanding learning environment would better prepare them for when they left the school.

I don't think the moral of this story needs too much explaining and it is something we all need to consider. When consider this from an emotional perspective, as always it is about getting the balance right and knowing when to 'comfort the disturbed' and 'when to disturb the comfortable'. Much of this book has been about getting an emotionally rich environment; subsequently a pedagogy of discomfort is one where learners move outside their comfort zones and are therefore challenged. The purpose is to challenge habits, practices and assumptions that we base our life around. This can only be done effectively in a well-supported emotional environment. Only through critically challenging many of the unfounded beliefs that most of us have, that guide our emotions and feelings, can we actually start to gain some understanding of our relationships and who we really are.

Advice

Engaging learners with pedagogy of discomfort

The table below is a way of helping you plan how and to what extent you will engage learners with pedagogy of discomfort. For example, in taking a topic such as friendships, as well as discussing all those areas that make us feel happy and content, by also going to the areas that can be slightly discomforting, ultimately empowers learners in the long run. Use the table to think about topics and how learners can be exposed to the discomfort zone in an emotionally supportive environment.

Topic	Comfort zone	Discomfort zone
friendship	friends make you feel good making new friends friends for life positive relationships expectations of friends	going separate ways feeling lonely feuds and falling out ending relationships feeling let down
1		
2		
3		
4		
5		
6		
7		
8		
9		

Application

Appendix 1

Match the emotion with the picture and discuss with students how they made the decision. What are the differences between some of the emotions when viewed by facial expressions, for example shocked and surprised?

1   2   3   4   5

6   7   8   9   10

Also, as part of extending learners' vocabulary – get them to list as many words associated with each picture as they can and try to get them to distinguish between each word. For example, image 1 could be described as happy or joyful – what is the difference?

Appendix 2

BASIS Model

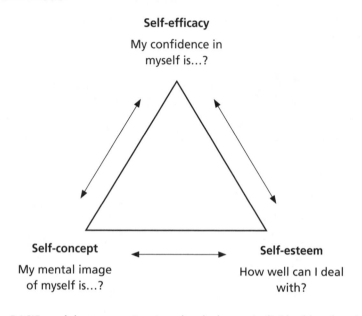

Self-efficacy

My confidence in
myself is...?

Self-concept

My mental image
of myself is...?

Self-esteem

How well can I deal
with?

The BASIS model can operate at a school, class or individual level and can be used as a focus for developing a positive self-image in children through the following principles on the opposite page.

- Creating a sense of **belonging** – in the sense of establishing a sense of community within a school or within a class, which includes values and celebrates with all its members.

- Creating a sense of **aspiration** – in the sense that the environment is one that recognizes and value aspirations through sharing clear and achievable targets.

- Creating a secure environment where learners feel **safe** – in that the learning environment is secure and emotionally safe, where diversity is valued and failure is regarded as a positive and essential accompaniment to a challenging environment.

- Creating an environment which values **identity** – in that the individuals that make up the environment are valued and where the relationship between self-esteem, self-efficacy and self-concept is central to personal development.

- Creating an environment that creates and values **success** – in that positive stocktaking is an essential feature of successful achievement, which will provide the platform for each student to develop their lifelong abilities and aim to perform to the best of those abilities.

Further reading

Antidote: Campaign for Emotional Literacy 5th Floor, 45 Beech St, Barbican, London, EC2Y 8AD. Tel 020 7588 5151. http://www.antidote.org.uk/

Dunbar, Robin, John Lycett and Louise Barrett (2005). *Evolutionary Psychology*, (Oneworld).

Goleman, Daniel (2005), *Emotional Intelligence*, (Bantam Books).

Goleman, Daniel (1999), *Working with Emotional Intelligence*, (Bloomsbury).

Haviland-Jones, Jeanette (2004) *Handbook of Emotions*, (Guilford Publications).

Nath Dwivedi, Kedar and Peter Brinley Harper (eds) (2004), *Promoting Emotional Well Being of Children and Adolescents and Preventing their Mental Ill Health*, (Jessica Kingsley).

The Social and Emotional Aspects of Learning (SEAL) http://www.teachernet.gov.uk

School of Emotional Literacy http://www.schoolofemotional-literacy.com/

Waters, Trisha (2004), *Therapeutic Storywriting: A Practical Guide to Developing Emotional Literacy in Primary Schools*, (David Fulton).

Whitehouse, Elaine and Warwick Pudney (1997), *A Volcano in My Tummy: Helping Children to Handle Anger: a Resource Book for Parents, Caregivers and Teachers*, (New Society).